Ebb Tide

Christine Fleming Heffner

*In the end nothing human is
alien to any of us, and old age is
humanity writ large.*

**Forward Movement Publications
Cincinnati**

SPIRAL

The green coil of years
like tendrils of the passion vine
clenches, strangles,
struggles upward to
whatever light there is.

C. F. H.

TABLE OF CONTENTS

ACKNOWLEDGMENTS

Most books begin with a section expressing the author's gratitude for human influences that have somehow blessed the writing, during it or before. This is for me an obligatory and rewarding part of writing the book.

I was taught to say "thank you" in my forming years (early forming years, I mean, since all our years are part of our forming). A lot of good teaching has since been shed like baby-teeth or has been abraded away by long living, but where I am aware of its fitness the need to give thanks has grown ever more urgent, for it is in recognizing what I have been given and in the response of gratitude that I am most aware of my membership in community, and of a belonging I sometimes despair of attaining.

Therefore I attempt what cannot be done well enough, and say "thank you" to many who (usually unknowing) have made this book possible. They can't be numbered, not all can be called by name, but some know who they are, and I want them to know that I do.

Most particularly I thank Ginny Robinson, who listened with patience and skill, and actually wanted to hear, over and over, through changings and re-writings. Many of her bits of wisdom are a part of the book. Over and above these things tower her caring, her recognition (in the truest sense), her needed affection.

I give ardent thanks to James and Sue Machan, for years of affection and caring, listening and responding.

I thank as well Charles Long, my editor, for eloquent encouragement and astonishing understanding, and this before we had met, at least face to face.

I must also say unheard thanks to many for whom this book and I will remain unknown, but who in the communion of artists (like the communion of saints) have been my mentors and support, in the time of this writing and as far into my past as memory goes. I bless their graces of language, heard and read even before I could comprehend meaning, from which I learned to recognize the human wonder that is literary art.

This book, like all human products, may have come into being by one set of hands, but it comes equally from myriad unknowing minds and hearts who dared to express what cannot be said but must be attempted.

The following works have been reprinted: from *The Living Church*— **Anamnesis, Dendrology, How Far?, Late Lesson, Prayer for a Cloud,** and **Triliteral**; from *Loaves and Fishes*—**Returning, This Day**; from *The*

Write Age—**A Long Time Later, Skeleton**; from *Big Rocks Trader*—**Sonora**; from *Bits and Pieces*—**This City of Houses**; from *Separate Doors*—**A Dwelling on the Postulates of the Science of Plate Tectonics**; from *The Spokesman*—**Nostrum**. **Summer Light** is reprinted from my book, *Reports from a Wilderness*.

INTRODUCTION: Why—and how—to read this book

Why another book about old age? Why not? The subject concerns us all, whenever we were born.

It concerns the young because (1), still far off, it is the future of their future, (2) the old are their fellow planetary residents, and (3) their own seniority is now being fashioned.

It concerns those in the busy middle years because the facts of old age impinge variously on their own lives, and because old age is their future, and getting closer.

It concerns those already undertaking elderhood. When you find yourself in something so complex, you need all the knowledge you can get. More, you need wisdom, which doesn't accompany arthritis and isn't conferred with retirement.

In the end, literally, nothing human is alien to any of us, and old age is humanity writ large.

Section I, THE VIEW FROM THE SHORE, talks about this part of life that is now so long it is spoken of as in three stages. Retirees find some of their peers are of another generation.

Section II, THE EDGE OF THE WATER, talks about how it feels to be old, when changes come thick and fast, in the world around and in oneself.

Section III, LEARNING TO FLOAT, talks about resources, external and internal. It offers some surprises about memory, some promises of learning, some cliches turned upside-down.

Because this book comes to the subject from several angles, it speaks with several voices, and in prose and poetry, each intended to do what it does best.

Think of the poems as verbal illustrations, though poetry is an auditory art. It should be heard. It is best to read it aloud, in order to savor the sounds, or to read silently at about the pace of speech, listening with your mind's ear.

Prose gives facts, subjects for thought, answers to problems. It is the medium of data and intellectual process. Beyond prose, this business of being human, at any age, is a matter of poetry, dealing with the indefinable and daring to confront mystery.

We live best, we understand deep things best, with our hearts and our senses as fully turned on as our heads, therefore . . .

Section IV, BEACHCOMBING, offers more poems, to be re-read, re-considered, allowed down into the reader's own experience, where live his/her hopes, fears, and sense of wonder.

The book, like an old man or woman, begins with fact and ends with question, begins with culture and ends in mystery, begins with prose and ends in poetry.

THE VIEW FROM THE SHORE

We look at old age from a busy shoreline. Who are those people, out where the ocean pulls away from here and now? What is it like to be old in this culture? Some things we thought we knew about old age turn out to be untrue.

MATTERS OF IDENTITY

Desert Varnish

I have a jade pendant I shaped and polished from a pebble I found at the edge of a Wyoming river. I treasure it because it tells me I sometimes have imagination and vision to see beneath the surface of things, I have the curiosity to question. In old age, these things are more precious than jade.

This rock, smaller than a quail egg, looked nothing like jade when I found it. It looked like the rock-colored, rock-shaped rocks around it, all encased in "desert varnish," but I took it home and put it to the grinding wheel.

"Desert varnish" is not a geologic term, but every western rockhound knows it—a hard coating, dun-colored or dark, that in dry climate forms on surfaces exposed to sun and wind. It streaks down cliffs where prehistoric peoples built stone cities. It covers scattered pebbles so they look alike, but under the varnish they vary. They may be petrified wood, granite, limestone, even (rarely, in the right places) jade. To see the real rock you must break it to see the fracture, or grind off the coating.

Forced into a kind of generic rockhood, such a coated pebble seems to have lost its identity. Its dramatic history is hidden: millennia of liquid magma later solidified and crystallized, or eons of successive sea-floor and risen land, perhaps the layering of sand deposits under shallow water. All the violence of crustal upheaval, of forming and breaking, and the stone's chemical make-up, its colors, everything interesting about it, have vanished.

The rocks look the same; under the varnish, each is unique. A pebble may be obsidian, brittle and translucent, or petrified wood, its living cells replaced by silica, or limestone with its freight of small bodies embalmed in calcium. Occasionally, it may be rarer, like that jade, with its toughness. Whatever the rock, it is disguised by desert varnish that hates natural difference. Yet the varnish itself is as much a product of nature as opening flower or erupting volcano. Knowing the rock takes curiosity, attention, imagination, patience, some learning. It takes effort, but it is worth it, whether gem material or not.

Sometimes old people acquire a "desert varnish," when natural processes seem to conspire to disguise the essential and unique person. We say a person "looks old," when we see a surface sameness and look no further. Even the old one himself, herself, may look in a mirror and say, "that isn't how I look. I'm still the same. Why do I look different?" It can be disheartening, this loss of one's image long lived with, the image in memory's mirror that defines one. Or used to.

Like the desert varnish, the change isn't as sudden as our perception of it, in ourselves or someone else. Before old age arrives, people have begun to acquire the desert varnish that hides their unique nature. At the onset of old age (whenever that may be) the individual begins to look to some observers like a generic "senior citizen." The process happens slowly; the result is seen suddenly.

How we think old age looks too often results from how it is shown by television and movies, by passing glances, by our own expectations. Too, the very depressed are hardly visible. The very active are so busy we don't include them in a category labelled "old." They are out here in the middle of the rest of us, doing their things.

Like the rocks, under an apparent sameness, people vary in their essential toughness, brittleness, and translucence. They differ in the metamorphoses of their history, changes brought about by the sun of many days, the winds of many events, the shaping of many emotions. Look under the surface.

Human singularity of character and personality is achieved as well as given, grown as well as molded. I suspect that the realized individual comes into being as the result of a lifetime of development, influence, and decision-making, with occasional spells of self-honesty and self-awareness if the person is brave and teachable. Yet human development is also *from* a given genetic makeup, the mental, physical, emotional and possibly spiritual characteristics acquired at conception. All things take place at least partly in response to and reaction against a changing environment. Becoming a human being is even more complex than becoming a jade pebble.

When you see old age, look deeper, as does the skilled photographer who sees the differences and reveals them by his art. Far from seeing "all alike," he knows the old to be his most variable and interesting subjects. There is character in old faces, meaning in old bodies, an artistry of time, circumstance, and the human spirit not given to rocks.

We decorate with bud and blossom, but we live by mature fruit, by grain ripened. If we see for ourselves rather than in cultural conformity, we will find in most of the old a beauty with life in it, fulfillment of the promise of spring shoot and summer flower.

It is not only that we need to look beneath a coating produced by environment. There is a unique beauty in the very weathering, in the mellowing and patina. We appreciate this in furniture but overlook it in people. It is a different kind of beauty from that screen and stage display, but it is beauty.

What appears to be sameness is individuality most observers don't see because they don't expect to see it. Youth is not all luscious skin and graceful movement, but we look for these and therefore find them. We look past the beauties of the old. By caring and knowing, by imagination, patience, and effort, we can find in any humanity uniqueness and beauty, worth beyond jewels.

The Semantics of Seniority

A lot of things begin to happen to people as they get older, and not all of them are necessary. They fall into a thorny patch called nomenclature. It may be "only a matter of semantics," except that semantics are seldom "only." Language is the tool we think with. Attitudes affect words, and then the words create attitudes. For instance, "youth," denotes a *time* of life, but the word is used as meaning a *quality* of life.

Do we, then, speak of the aged? the aging? the old?

"The aged" sounds like a state once and for all arrived at, as with wine and cheese. By the time people are "aged" we aren't quite sure what has happened, or when, and the effects don't seem to add to value, attractiveness, or, if you will, flavor. People don't suddenly get to an "aged stage." The processes of life are continuous. People are ag*ing*, but since this is ongoing, it is something everybody is doing. The "preemie" in the intensive-care nursery and the centenarian mentioned in the newspaper are both aging. To say that one is aging is simply to say that time is going by and he or she is living in it.

Why don't we use "elders" now? The word implies wisdom and good judgment; it even confers status. It also carries religious connotations, and that may be its drawback. Maybe we lost it when we adopted "young" as the only legitimate compliment. "You're such a young elder" sounds as ridiculous as it is.

The connotations of the word "old" mean that the only way to compliment people who *are* old is to tell them they are *not*. Once the rite of passage is observed—retirement, Social Security card, moving to the Sun Belt—everything complimentary is summed up in "you look young." You can look charming at 75, but not young. Old and attractive are not mutually exclusive adjectives, but once past middle-age, "young" is the only compliment one is likely to get, false as it is. Maybe that's the worst part of the lie: It leaves other compliments unsaid. It is the generic accolade. One size fits all. And says nothing meaningful to any.

And what on earth is it OK to *call* them?

"Aged," "aging," "old"—why do we shy away from them all? "Senior citizens" is routine, but I can't see what citizenship has to do with age, once people are old enough to vote. Maybe it started as implied assurance that these people still had enough wits left to mark a ballot.

For me, "seniors" has better vibes than other words, and it's honest and straightforward. Most of us have been "seniors" before in some different context. But this still leaves unanswered the question of how to refer to the aging process.

In Western culture the general rule about wines, furniture, and fossils is: the older the better. Those things don't die (except fossils, who did it too long ago to matter), and this is a culture terrified of death, for all that death so pervades its entertainment. Death isn't so much a taboo as an embarrassment, but old age is too close to it in most minds to be comfortable. People will cross the street to avoid having to deal with the subject, as many a recent widow can testify. Nobody knows the right thing to say to the bereaved, and, by extension, to anyone whose years are evidencing physical inroads. That, too, is *memento mori*. The usual solution is to pretend nothing is happening, which of course is nonsense. People write to etiquette columns to ask what is the "right" thing to say, as if there were a rune to make all well. There isn't.

What helps verbally, in either case, is no socially accepted formula, certainly not what is bright and/or original, but the simplest and the most truly intended—things like, "I'm sorry," to the bereaved, and "I'm glad to see you" to the old. If one is.

A Demographic Oddity—the New Generation

A major portion of today's old people are a demographic oddity. The increasing longevity of Americans has put an added generation in place, but this generation is not, as you might assume, tacked onto the end of life. The added generation is the next-to-last one. It is as if you had cut the deck and stuck this bunch in before the bottom cards in the stack.

Those in their late eighties and nineties are roughly the equivalent in physical, mental, and social condition to the sixty and seventy-year-olds of two or three decades ago. The present sixty and seventy-year-olds are the new kids on the block. We haven't inherited any "proper" social attitudes to them. Nor have

7

they. Newcomers are often touchy, and these tend to be.

How do you wind down an active, thinking, effective life?

These people lack earlier examples of well-lived old age. They have no handed-down concepts of this age, they have no role models except what they see on the screen, wide or home-size, and those are seldom applicable.

Members of this new generation may be brave, distraught, emotionally disoriented, even seriously depressed, or they may be the vivacious and debonair who are wondering what has happened, to them and to those who address them. Even the vivacity may be only force of habit putting them through the motions, when the energy is running down, but it's the only style they know.

Some of these people *are* depressed (more about that later—a lot more, it needs consideration). If it ever happened to them before, it at least happened in a familiar structure, usually in minds and bodies that felt more capable and self-assured than now.

You don't hear much about "second childhood" any more, yet that is where these seniors are, in some ways, but it isn't what used to be meant by that. It surely isn't the repeat of a healthy childhood, but more like the state of children who are given toys and games and television but little attention. It is going back to a place where you have to ask permission a lot, wait until things are convenient for someone else, and get entertained, rather than stimulated. As children do, these adults need to learn, explore, make relationships. Most especially, they need to be given attention. Sometimes they feel rather invisible.

Being a new generation is more distressing than you might think, because the lack of cultural carry-over hits right when the carry-over from personal pasts seem to be fading out. These people are perforce retiring, moving out of houses, out of known geography, becoming single, and otherwise undergoing radical changes of life-style.

Sometimes it is the most self-sufficient and capable who suddenly say to themselves, "but I know how to cope. I am a person who can do things, who can handle my life. Only now I can't seem to." This can be incapacitating; it can lead to quiet desperation, kept secret. It isn't the complainers who concern me, but those who smile shyly, say in quiet voices, "I'm just fine," and spend a lot of time alone in their rooms.

They may suffer an "I have no right to complain" syndrome, thinking that since their material needs are met they shouldn't want anything else. They may be "counting their blessings," forgetting that invisible and uncounted damages still hurt. They are children of their culture, which is technologically rich and philosophically destitute. They have the *things* that used to seem important. What else is there to want?

What they need now is a philosophy of life that has little to do with material things, but these are people who seldom think in philosophical terms. How could they? Who ever taught them to? In this culture, say "philosophy" and hearers will think "theoretical vagueness." Yet it is our philosophy, values, beliefs that determine our concrete and objective lives. There is no need to choose between the philosophic and what we call the "real." That's like asking which leg we need most. (This, too, will get further consideration in ensuing pages.)

A philosophy of life is something their churches should have been offering them, I think, but I don't see many churches doing that. Rules, yes; philosophy, no. Churches tend to teach that your worth depends on what you do for others. Is anybody shifting gears? Shouldn't they?

These people are understandably confused. Like teenagers, they find that when they want to be thought capable, they get treated as if they were incompetent, but when they need help and understanding, they are expected to be self-sufficient. The difference is that the adolescent can look to the future to solve his confusion; the senior suspects it will only get worse.

The new generation is only one piece of what is the largest segment of this population. It is the beginning of "old age," a time extending for three or more decades, so large a sector that it is spoken of now in "thirds." Professionals refer to the very oldest as the "third third," to the new generation as the "first third." No one seems sure whether this is the beginning of the end or the end of the beginning. I think of these as the junior seniors.

The market-place is aware of these demographics as its opportunities. New industries spring up to offer the "new old" goods and services which may—often may not—make the shift easier. Chief among these are retirement housing (fortunately, a far cry from what was once called the "old folks' home") and health insurance.

The retirement housing complex is such a new concept that it is still creating its own confusions as it develops. In theory, often in reality, it is an answer to problems of beginning old age, but it, too, has no precedents, and must find its way by trial and error. It seems to me that often what is intended for the still active and healthy who want to shed burdens of home-keeping, soon does turn into a new and expensive version of the "old folks home." Those who enter such senior housing while self-sufficient, neither needing nor wanting to be totally cared for, don't always stay that way. My observation has left me questioning whether they stay that way as well as they might elsewhere. Other entrants, from the start, need more support than they think they do. The whole matter of congregant living is an evolving process. It does provide for a need, but it also does present difficulties. What *is* "home," anyway? (More of that later, too. It's another big subject.)

As for the attention of the insurance industry to the needs (and finances) of seniors, this has become a matter of serious concern. Seniors are understandably anxious about future medical needs. Costs escalate, and who other than a mathematical genius with a crystal ball can tell whether current insurance coverage is adequate? There are many experts around, offering advice on the subject, but they are also usually selling insurance, which makes their helpfulness suspect.

In spite of warnings against scams, many old people are being victimized. Not all insurance vendors are trustworthy, some are aggressive, persistent, and even threatening. (Believe it. I've been threatened.)

Many retirees have a good deal of disposable income, are unsure of this strange new world, and don't know how to prepare for their future. Being this new generation, for many, feels surprisingly shaky. In some ways shaky is exactly what it is.

Medicare, long assumed to provide for medical needs in old age, has become a political football, which doesn't make for feelings of security. As for Social Security, this provision for old age financial stability seems to exhibit a tendency to melt. It was never meant to furnish total support for retirement, but this gets forgotten.

Old age is for most a time of reduced energy and expanded knowledge, disadvantages of diminishments, advantages of experience. Especially are these losses and gains the resources and tests for living in the "first third." I see these people tending to overestimate their physical abilities and underestimate their mental and spiritual ones, or underuse them.

The Unbelonging

This "first-third" time is the making of a new life, which most have done before, but they seldom did it alone. Now it can feel very alone, especially in a new location, for while residents in retirement communities have immediate access to others of their kind, that is only true if by "their kind," you mean members of their age-group. For many (I suspect most) this group membership gives little communication and can be depersonalizing. Those from 60 years old to 90 are of at least two generations. Many who are thrown together in this one basket don't really speak the same language, except for polite pleasantries in hallways. That is true even when they haven't displaced themselves to a new section of the country, and that is a frequent situation.

Things people normally share—hobbies, social concerns, politics, skills—are not age-limited. Until retirement, one's peers are selected by interests, knowledge, attainments, social conventions, and experience. Moving into retirement housing can be like going off to school, but without letters from home.

This residence ought to be a "safe place," in which to make new attachments. Ideally it ought to become a new community, or a new version of community, but it is not that easy. In the real world, community is forged by working or learning together, by sharing responsibilities, in school, business, neighborhood, family. It takes a strong (if invisible) coherence of attention and concern, in order to make a community. It is seldom created by the sharing of buildings and schedules, even if they include entertainment. Community is not the same thing as "togetherness."

Add to that a really severe deprivation that can happen, unnoticed by the world and usually unexpected by seniors. It is one of the two most devastating events of this period. This is loss of the automobile. The other is death of a spouse.

Freedom of movement is, in this culture, a basic one, lost when the car keys are turned over to someone else. The automobile is, like the dollar, more than symbol. It *is* what it symbolizes.

How do you do your thing—maybe new things you need to do now—without being able to move about? How do get to "belong" in a new community? How do you find spiritual sustenance without a church *of your choice?* How do you serve your current needs, much less your wants, without *spontaneous* access to transportation? Use of public transportation, at best, requires more walking than many seniors can do comfortably, even safely. Weather can pose more problems for seniors than for others. In old age, there are many gradations of what can still be called "good health."

More may depend on transportation than even seniors are aware, until they deal with it. How do they continue cultural interests and memberships, fill educational wants or needs, how will they seize opportunities, keep friendships and established concerns, find new ones? The car is not only a car. It is library, the arts, shopping, museums, friendships, escape from the urban.

Retirement is usually a time of adjusting to a new place

(literally and figuratively) and new lifestyle, forfeiting independence. A big chunk of the self-sufficiency you've taken for granted rolls away on the tires of what was once your car.

It Works Both Ways

Yet to say all these true things is also to be misleading, for this last stage is no more monolithic than any other. It may be less so, since the old are more individuated than younger people. Their circumstances are less alike. All human beings need to be seen one by one, rejoicing and suffering in their own ways, being puzzled by their unique lives. The old may most need to be seen individually, but they are less likely to be.

Not all the old are needy in the same ways; not all are justifiably called needy. Some are severely deprived in unnoticed ways, and these, the invisibly needy, must not be overlooked.

This relationship of the old and the rest of us doesn't face in one direction. Needs don't exist only on one side of it. The old merit society's concern, but society also badly needs them. They are the nation's, the world's, store of experience and possible wisdom, they are our links with all that is past. They are, still, where our humanity came from, and comes from.

In them reposes a history of events that make us, as a people, what and who we are. They are a history that will cease to be accessible when it is not a living one.

"They are a history that will cease to be."

ARCHEOLOGY

-a-

There's something in us wants to make
    for the sake only of making
then something that wants to make
    what is made continue
long past the maker, all the makers,
    the very kind who make.
We resist the breaking down, not only ours,
    wage everlasting war against
what forbids all everlasting,
    become conservators to monuments.

Yet in a counterforce to making
    we want to smash, to bring to nothing
what cannot last forever, perhaps because
    it cannot last forever, but longer than we.
We make, but cannot make endure, because
    what survives is only what we make,
not our made selves, so easily shattered.
    We punish, imputing survival guilt
to what cannot know the guilt we know.

-b-

In these walls is diminishing treasure,
    left of a history,
time-span of horror and mystery, locked
    in threatened images, a communal epic
where things that have been seen
    can be shown only in metaphor,

14

where things that have been heard,
  anguish and triumph and disaster,
  can echo in innocent minds
  to be screamed again, sobbed forever,
where things that were touched and are dust
  can take their shapes again
  out of body-blessed earth
  and earth-damned ashes
  and shadows cast by air.

We dig with precise and unaccustomed patience
  ancient graves, on our knees praying
with careful brushes and sieves, to be granted
  remains of our past, a thread here
there a rusted rivet, hint of carved pattern
  while pages of record lie
crumpled in bone walls where the old keep them,
  some who may not remember Tuesday
but in whom a vanished time burns clear,
  legible briefly in consuming flame.

-c-

Unwilling to be old, unable to be young
  so many lost in the unexpected,
a time without purpose, unknowing its worth.
  We reach back, back. We might resist onward,
come to the state of crumbling statues
  nobody knows where to store.

A bustling world doesn't know us, need us.
  We think we don't need ourselves.
The world of our own hearts cries
  over long-spilt blood and emptied dreams,
forgetting while we can still weep, while
  we can fear, there is yet a tomorrow
where we can bring yesterdays to be valued
  though they cannot take us home.

15

"I'm still the same . . . Why do I look different?"

IMAGE

I try to copy my own reflection
without mirrors. They distort,
try to sell me a lying reverse,
lack a whole dimension.
I want somewhere a true image,
maybe engraved under my skin,
safe from time's abrasion, a place
where going through the world
doesn't twist it, an honest image
where I can find it when
I start to believe in mirrors.

OLD AGE IN CONTEXT

Complexities of the Here and Now

Not long ago, *Modern Maturity* printed contradictory letters to the editor. One expressed annoyance at "bouncing, hyperactive seniors" seen in the magazine; the second spoke of the magazine's presentation of the old in terms of a "lack of vitality."

Of course, old age is neither inevitable suffering and incompetence nor constant activity. Extremes exist, but they don't give a realistic picture of the last part of life. Old age includes a whole spectrum of human nature and experience. Most of that experience happens somewhere in the middle.

Like the second writer, I don't want the old shown as tired, boring, decrepit. Like the first, I don't think healthy seniors must be constantly moving, physically or otherwise. Needed here, I think, is the classical beginning of fruitful discussion: Define your terms. What does "active" mean? This culture sees vitality and achievement as material, then uses those to measure human value. "What is his net worth?" is a financial question. "You are so active" refers to visible involvements.

I wish publications for and about the retired would give us examples who are intellectually acute, emotionally and spiritually aware individuals, who find personal fulfillment even when physical energy is reduced. I would like to read about men and women who use lifetimes of experience to help make the most of the present, people who know and use their resources, who show compassion for those with less, who learn from those who have more. I would like to see the multiple riches of old age, but our printed words reflect the culture, which is reductionist. The pervasive question seems to be: "Is this all there is?"

Life holds so many potentialities that only a mere fraction

can be realized in a single lifetime. I think what I want to see is summed up in the word "wisdom," but that was never an *automatic* result of living a long time. It has to be worked at; it always did. I would like to see how some achieve it.

Old Age Is Not What It Used To Be (but maybe it never was!)

Those who plunge or slide or stumble into old age now must do their learning by trial and error. Definitions are slippery; few former precepts still apply. There are few personal role models, public ones tend to the extremes those letters decried.

In earlier times one watched well-known individuals grow old, so what was seen was a process, not a caste. It was a familiar one, taking place in the neighborhood and the family.

There Went the Neighborhood

It is a truism that we are a nomadic culture, but I have yet to hear much discussion of the results of this, or of ways in which we might deal with it.

Being nomads affects everyone, starting with the young. Children no longer spend years with schoolmates in one place, the same people slowly changing and differing from one another. Now they must adjust to a succession of new places and new faces, in a culture consisting of sets of peers. It sometimes looks as if children, adolescents, young adults, the middle-aged, and the old are different species living tangential lives, so groups see one another only *as groups,* i.e., by category. A whole society seems to be turning itself into living proof of the fact that "separate but equal" doesn't allow relatedness, and never stays equal very long. The old are the least visible category.

Ageism, like all categorical perceptions, comes from looking without seeing, without vision. We need a kind of wide-angle vision in order to see relationships; we need a telescopic vision to see individuals. We even need a kind of microscopic vision to discover exquisite details, things not obvious to common sight. Learning to know other people has never been an easy curriculum, but it is basic for our species. It may have been simpler when you needed only occasionally to integrate a few new characters into a continuing cast. Now our life's *dramatis personae* shifts often, and nobody is on stage long enough for children to find out who is worth trusting or learning from. In our lived drama, type-casting you might say, is standard.

Like much modern theater, the pace of our lives doesn't give much chance for involvement in the characters. Is this a reason why so many moderns find it hard to make attachments, why they feel alarm at the prospect of real intimacy, when a superficial intimacy is so easy? These young who are afraid of closeness are the children and grandchildren of the present old, and they find it hard to deal with relics of a past they know so little about. Opportunities for interaction are few, and mostly artificial.

There is often a significant language barrier between generations, more distancing even than the age difference. The young have always altered language, but I think I remember them being more culturally bilingual.

Now there are more old people, but families live further away from them. They are not members of whole households, certainly they don't live intimately in households. Usually they are "out there" somewhere, back in one of the last towns the family lived in or in retirement houses or apartments. They may be visited occasionally, but they are not part of the neighborhood, or what's left of it. Which brings us to another fact of current culture.

Family Matters

The family isn't what it used to be, either. Even the extended family some can remember was a reduction from the earlier clan and tribe and community. In the recent past, a "standard" family of two parents and a few siblings has shrunk to a family of a parent and child or two. Just when it might have been a help (if also sometimes inconvenient) to have quasi-parental figures around, it became less possible. Houses aren't big enough to let any of the "extended family" (if you have one) into the living arrangements. There is no day-by-day contact.

With second and third marriages, families began to re-expand, but into a form that, at best, challenges relationship. Sibling conflict is ancient (see *Genesis* for fratricide) but siblings used to share a history. Members of a married-again family share no past, good or bad, and deal with new sources of rivalry and mistrust. Relationships between generations are mostly strained or non-existent. They may be only "half-kin" anyway.

Meanwhile, all involved are nomads, which compounds any difficulties. We are a nation of wanderers, but without the built-in adaptations to wandering that historically nomadic peoples have. Traveling as tribes, extended families, they take their human environment with them. We travel with very small tents. Human support is only where we find it. The prospect of leaving again keeps us from making deep relationships anywhere, from finding support systems as we go from place to place.

Historically conditioned nomads move in coherent clusters, we splinter ours. Their old are a vital part of the coherence; in our splintered groups, the old get left behind somewhere, so our nomadism affects the relationships of generations. Children don't see individuals who are their grandparents; grandparents don't get to know children as the changing persons they are. You can only know well the grandchildren you have interacted with as they raced through childhood. There are surely exceptions, but generally a geography gap seriously widens any generation gap.

The isolation, often instability, of the average American family impinges on all its members. Just when they are living longer and keeping healthier, the old are more remote and less intimately known than ever. When family members live distant they are more easily categorized. This is no trivial matter.

Lost in the Outer Categories

Categories are closed boxes, their contents invisible; this obviates insight, and in both directions. Categorical thinking judges, but cannot understand; being the object of it creates resentment, and the process is reciprocal.

Categorization always rests, as on granite, on the assumption that "they" are all alike. The familiar "I can't tell them apart" says more about the looker than the looked-at. To say it about the old is particularly silly, they being more highly individuated than the young. Teaching students over sixty, I found them more varied in personality than any younger ones I knew.

The very young I've known varied greatly, too. I suspect it is in adolescence that people tend to "clump," with teen uniforms a symptom, but that life tends to crumble sameness in old age.

When the old are mentally stored in category boxes, it is easy to believe one of two stereotypes of old age: one the frail and incompetent, to be somehow housed until death brings relief (to whom?), and the other the social and/or political activist. Neither is a norm. I think either picture, *per se,* is unfair to all in the community, and not least to the old. The view of old age as automatic incompetence robs everyone of delight and enrichment, frightens those who are younger, and forces upon the old themselves a feeling of alienation, a lowered sense of their value. These can result in the depression often misperceived as "senile dementia."

Older Americans are beginning to constitute a huge subculture, separated from the larger inclusive culture to the detriment of both. Like most subcultures, it contains human tragedy and comedy, an infinity of aspects of the human condition. There seem to be two categories of seniors, overlapping only slightly. There are old couples. There is a vastly larger population of old single persons, predominantly women. When an old couple is divided by death, the widowed member, in time, becomes one of the senior singles, but there is a most painful distance to be covered in that becoming. Is this culture's population in other age groups so separated?

It is difficult to find what old age is like until you get there, for we are presented mostly stereotypes. Where, in print, entertainment, or social experience do we find the still-competent but frail widow or widower, coping with small losses, diminished energy, minor physical disability? Where is the partially dependent and beloved grandmother, where is the community's "elder statesman" who lends a cool head and calm advice to family or group or organization? Where is the old person who is so much himself/herself that achievements and social roles are left behind, whose friendships and regard come now simply from character and personality?

Where are the volunteers giving as they can but winning no competitions? Where is the retired teacher who still teaches as opportunity and need ask, whose offered skills are unnoticed but vital? Where is the spouse coping with his or her personal changes as well as baffling changes in the partner? Where is the retired business-woman caring for parents, or the one who, because of hers, can't retire? Where is the widower learning household skills with courage and humor, the widow learning to use tools inherited from a husband? These are not roles, but persons. None represents old age, but they all live in it.

Glowing brochures show us residents of retirement communities, but not what is happening to them. And in them. For all the glossy photographs, life in these places is not just golf and swimming and gourmet meals. The sunny walls don't keep out pain, illness, death, loss, fear, alcoholism, even divorce. Grass on the greens grows well; what growing goes on in minds and hearts?

Old human beings, in their multitudinous variations, are remarkable in their sometimes heroic ability to undergo pain and loss, and still function with competence, even with joy and the giving of joy, still to live with class. They are remarkable, too, for unexpressed emotional pain that might be eased.

The stage of life makes difference, but precise chronology doesn't. I met a friend who seemed to lack his usual crusty affability. When asked what was the matter, he roared: "What is the matter with me? Yesterday at 2:15 p.m., senility set in." He had just been retired as professor at a prestigious university. He knew his classical languages and his teaching skills as well that day as he had the week before. If he felt suddenly less valued, it was his culture who made the point.

No doubt there must be points of change and rites of passage, but let's not give them more meaning than they have. If one is incompetent at seventy, he may have been becoming so at forty-seven; if he is a bore, he likely always was.

Except for inroads of disease or trauma, old age seems to make us what we always were, but more so. It can make us more crabby and critical, but also more intense, more interesting, more worth knowing. Old age is a time when individuality develops, if we will let it, and also when we are more willing to let that individuality show. Old age is not really being past your prime, but moving into a different kind of "prime."

There are exceptions. Of two women close to me, one who had been always compulsively independent suddenly crumbled when autonomy was lost. The other, who had been often demanding and dependent, became a charming person, a delight to be around.

The change in the first came with serious disease, fear and pain. Those are not necessarily results of old age.

The public attitude to old age is improving. Seldom is it still seen as the trash-bin of life, with inevitable loss of dignity. Well, maybe it would be truer, if more cynical, to say it has been noticed how much political clout is wielded by the sheer size of the older population, and how much expendable income some of its members have.

Very active old age gets a good press ("news" still being the unusual), but is an old person only interesting if she breaks a record, if he racks up the most hours of volunteer work? Is competitiveness still the criterion, until the grim reaper wins?

That competitiveness, so general that it goes home from office and school and playground, also gets moved into retirement housing. It is a constant in our society, everywhere a source of tension and fatigue, as well as motivation. The old know very well that there is seldom any way they are going to be "number one," and in this world, if you are not number one you aren't even in the game (even if it isn't a game). Is "winning" really everything? Or are we trying to "win" in a lot of situations that are not contests? Can old people enjoy life when they stop competing? For that matter, *can* they stop competing? What does that say about the rest of us, for that matter?

The need to be number one is undoubtedly closely allied to the cult of perfection we live in, and live by. The need to be "perfect" is a sure road to anxiety, and often to depression. Anxiety and depression are the cultural epidemics of our time. In old age, earlier anxieties may be replaced by a new cluster of fears, all relating to future loss: loss of control, of oneself or others, loss of autonomy, loss of dignity, competence, mobility. There is fear of forced conformity and of pain. One of the chief anxieties is that old people will be burdens to their children.

For many, feared losses are already taking place, by catastrophe or, more often, by a slow erosion. The fear of loss of competence finds its half-joking way into conversation as reference to loss of memory. Every human being forgets a name or a fact occasionally. When the old do it, they may assume it comes from something terrible and irreversible, and they cringe while they joke about it. It is no joke, but it also is not inevitably a dire symptom. A lost name is no sign of approaching disaster, but the anxiety of an assumption can cause forgetfulness.

A study reported by Health & Fitness News Service found that seniors given a story to remember and tell to children did better than younger subjects, though they had done poorly when given random numbers to memorize. Testers theorized that we may remember important things better as we age. I suspect we simply find "random" information not worth processing.

Depression, the other epidemic, is frighteningly pervasive, and often diagnosed as something else. What was long called "senile dementia" may be only evidence of combined depression, medication, faulty nutrition, sedentary life, and/or emotional trauma. There is remarkably little knowledge about the action of drugs in the aging body, and not much known about its nutritional needs. Too often, dosage is based on the action of drugs in younger bodies, though serious metabolic changes take place in the old. Geriatric medicine is a recent specialty, so far it offers few specialized teaching sources. Much research is needed, and ongoing education for physicians already long in practice.

Sometimes the source of depression is—depression. There is a real difference between this illness and sadness or grief. This *is* an illness; sadness is the organism's appropriate response to stimuli, grief a normal physical and emotional coping mechanism. This culture tends to see only happiness and "adjustment" as healthy, but the truth is otherwise. The suppression of awe, wonder, curiosity, and the urge to explore places or ideas, is a chief sign of depression, but may also be a cause of it.

The healthy psyche is self-protective. When threatened or injured it fights, flees, adapts, or schemes. The depressed psyche feels helpless and hopeless, simply undergoes ("suffers" in the old sense and the current one) whatever is happening.

We know that babies deprived of human interaction fail to thrive. So do adults. From birth, a child needs attention, stimulus, response, nurture, caring, new experience, and it will still need these when grown. Usually, adults can manage to get them. In old age, as family-related and work-related relationships are broken, as emotional ties are broken by death or geographical displacement, as people receive less attention, are touched and listened to less, are removed from familiar patterns of life, those basic needs reappear.

Some sense of this need, some sense that we have become remote from one another, has resulted in the fact that it's now expected that we hug strangers, and that the use of first name is almost required, even in business telephone calls.

As symbolic gestures, these hugs are surely helpful but they can't go deep enough to fill really basic needs. It must be noted that they can even be painful reminders of the real superficiality of one's remaining relationships. Gestures of intimacy in the absence of true intimacy can be deadly, and surely as artificial as any Victorian code of manners.

Culture seems "natural" when we are in the middle of it, but we can be astonished later at what we have put up with. I suspect that in years to come we will be aghast at some of our taken-for-granted false familiarity. It is most likely to be uncomfortable to those whose deeply familiar things are fast passing away.

Seniors don't just have a problem of how others see them. A worse one is that of how they see themselves. Old people may be housed apart, in a kind of benign *de facto* version of *apartheid,* but they are not immune to their culture's attitudes, virtues, and vices. Sometimes they are extreme examples.

Having and Being

Some psychologist-philosophers suggest that human life is lived in the three modes of having, doing, and being, each a leg in a psychic triangle, and that most people's lives make very uneven triangles. In twentieth-century culture, *having* and *doing* get the most attention, and they interact. Having requires doing, doing necessitates more having.

What does it mean to have and do less in a world where people are defined by what they visibly have and do?

How much concern and attention goes to *being?* A possible advantage of old age is that by the time people get there, they may have learned how to "be." The *having* is vulnerable to those years, its loss may be painful, but it isn't disaster if the *being* is strong enough. The *doing* may have to diminish, but this can be weathered. It may even be profitable, sometimes a relief.

Depression in old age may come from a loss of the sense of worth we tied to the having and doing. A senior who has invented, delighted, built, defended, or nurtured, if those around him now know nothing of it, may feel it "doesn't count."

If *doing* is the only manifestation of vitality this society can see, if *having* is the only potent symbol of value, how does it recognize *being, becoming*? How does anyone learn them?

Do human beings take this amazing voyage we call life, only to arrive at a dead end called "old age?" Or is old age a place where *becoming* is evidenced, freshly visible when the clutter of having and the busy-ness of doing are cleared away?

Maybe in old age, a person is like the magnificent sculpture of the winter tree, when leaves and flowers have fallen away. Those were not the tree. It is when foliage no longer covers it that the tree is visible, the more beautiful for its loss. The leaves existed to serve this; this didn't exist to produce leaves.

Western culture is a long way from seeing age by such a metaphor. Even the most "positive" view of old age looks to those who, in the tree metaphor, are evergreens, their being obscured by what they have and do, until it all goes at once. These are the old ones who keep moving, no matter the direction, who keep "active," sometimes a geriatric version of the hyperkinetic child.

Maybe the deciduous senior tree is a true model for the human condition, where loss of energy may offer the gift of simplicity in which live contemplation, philosophy, love of beauty, unity with nature. These are things of which in youth we are deprived by much-doing and much-having.

Perhaps Americans are most comfortable with *doing* because, while action demands decision and courage, it demands less of either than does *being*. The courage to *be* must come from the whole person—mind, body, emotion, spirit.

Life is lived by trade-offs. We do and have at the expense of becoming, but it is doing and having that are external and vulnerable. No definition of humanity is adequate. It is natural, it nevertheless is mystery, but the rest of nature is also mystery, kin to those who respond to it, kind to those who pay it the homage of attention and respect.

America is hooked on numbers, no doubt an appeal of lottery and stock market and Las Vegas. Numbers seem real and solid, while so much of life is hard to define. Yet it is the numbers that are artificial, numbers that can be juggled to seem what they are not. This is a fact con men live by.

Ours is a society in which few things count unless you can count them. Both "young" and "old" are quantitative adjectives, but in this culture, they take on qualitative meaning. We all know jaded, spiritually flabby young people and eager, curious, old ones; if we see these as mere exceptions, we retain the stereotypes. Maybe we think of them as exceptions *in order to* retain the stereotypes, because those are comfortable. People hate to give them up, because then they have to pay attention, they have to think, they may have to admit they were wrong.

The stages of a human life can't be sharply delineated by figures. A person is not defined by an age. Legal maturity is defined by a birthday, but human maturity isn't. Humans go through the stages of life similarly, but not by the numbers.

"Is old age a place where becoming is . . . freshly visible?"

BECOMING

*All my life I was becoming who I am but
in the business of living a lot of me got lost.
The best things I did were often those I did
when I didn't know what I was doing.*

*Youth was so sure it frightens me, looking back,
at my idle brain and over-reckoned wisdom.
It can happen yet, for my youth continues —
possibility, under the weight of days.*

*Maybe I never am, but am always almost.
Can that explain the itch, the hunting after
what wasn't there when I found it, finding
what I didn't know I was looking for?*

*What do we know? We are born and we live and we die.
These may be the only things forbidden knowing.
A bird flying, scent of cedar, sound of a bell
may be what tell us more than any knowledge.*

*Is old age release from duty-directed years
to find the child I am, like a lost sister?
Then how do I knock down bars no longer there,
burst out of bandages, get back to becoming?*

"We are a nation of wanderers. "

THIS CITY OF HOUSES
(an architecture of the heart)

This small apartment is full of houses — for example,
the home I said I could only leave by amputation,
that place where friendship grew,
and romance still — or again — burned bright.
But I am here and it feels like home.
You are not here. You were no longer there.
That was the amputation.
                +++
The fervent double-colored roses
that graced the place where we ate, we talked,
bloom within my eyes and will last as long as I do.
The French love seat has come along again.
I don't know where our bed is. The desk
where I wrote hasn't followed. The writing has,
and includes you always, somehow.
                +++
Furniture trails for a while, but sooner or later
drops by the wayside, or follows the children away.
I lost the big round table that lived in our kitchens,
and your chair, the piano whose keys the cat jumped on,
and the bicycles. They must all be somewhere, but you
have outlasted them. Your voice I still hear,
the way I still see the roses.
                +++

Other houses are here, one attic-furnished
where our first-born walked, windows framing a mountain,
a tent lost to desert, where I spent the seasons
schooling eyes and ears. Dim are the houses
I existed in while you survived bloody Europe,
bright a maple's upper branches where we lunched.

      + + +

So it is in these little dwelling places
where people settle, after long living.
This is a city, because its walls
hold houses — great, small, loved in.
Eyes that see vanished roses see those homes
wood, stone, brick, now invisibly built
of memory, of loss and loving beyond it.

      + + +

I inhabit all the places I have left. No,
they are in me, here where I keep awake,
missing our compromises, our matching likes,
music, books, rocks, the loveseat and the house.
As a bird shapes her nest, I shuffle this to fit,
in this city of vanished houses that still shelter.

MATTERS OF PERCEPTION

The Place to Grow Old In

In the recent past, seniors often chose to stay in their homes all their lives. This, perhaps a problem for others, made things good for the chooser. The familiar setting not only let them be "at home" where they were, it must have made playing the last act simpler, made cues easier to remember and kept events part of the drama as a whole.

It's true that everyone dies alone, but a long-lived-in home as stage for it provides earlier characters in supporting roles, possibly echoing some of their lines. The curtain was always in place, and there are remembered exits and entrances.

More and more, though staying in one's own house may be preferable, it isn't practical. For single widows, familiar comforts are strained by anxiety and frustration. The upkeep of a house calls for strength and know-how. Once there were neighbors, extended families included those who could help, but that was an ideal, not always a reality.

Today's answer to "where?" often means joining the migration to retirement housing, in strange places where one's children live. Sometimes the parents feel rather like lemmings.

The stage is new, the scenery changed, the play seems to have been re-written. Maybe it's a different play. Commercial or organizational retirement complexes offer answers, but, like modern science, raise new ones. The move to such a place usually means loss of long-established social, emotional, even practical, support systems, right when they are most needed.

Even eagerly anticipated retirement may bring a surprising nostalgia, for people with whom one shared the work-place, for instance. Sometimes having the children near is more romantic than effective; they may be only geographically closer.

Role Reversals

At best, they are not still children. They have changed, as they should, and so have parents. Expectations may lead to disappointment. Children's lifestyles can disturb parents whose values are affronted. Sometimes very active seniors bewilder the children. ("They're getting out of the box! They're loose!" seems to be the reaction.) Sometimes your children are now as sure they know it all as you were when you were their mother.

Finally, in a supposedly "natural" reversal of roles, grown children try to take over decision-making for parents who can make their own, but even those who can't may want to anyway. Along with their parents' physical problems, children may assume mental impairment, but real inability is frustrating enough, and what seems (or is) condescension is insulting.

I think whoever brought forth this "role-reversal" concept opened a can of fairly poisonous worms. Even when age-related deterioration is all too real, and care needed like that of small children, these parents are *not* children of their children. Grown children can't know their parents as the persons they are. (Or probably ever were.) On both sides of the equation lie distorted perceptions, selective memories, unreal hopes, buried resentments and guilts. No matter how needful, a ninety-year-old parent is not really like a year-old child, or a nine-year-old.

The geographic move is booby-trapped. Retired parents and working children operate on different time-schemes. Visits which feel frequent to children are perceived as all too occasional by parents in their unaccustomed leisure, often in their loneliness.

It is often assumed that children may find parents boring, but this is frequently reversed. The old have no patent on memory-lapses; memories that don't agree with your own can be frustrating. If a factually shared history is too differently sensed, the door is opened to blame, guilt, hurt feelings, resentments or, finally, emotionally-loaded silence.

Dear friendships, too, change over years, often—not always—for the better. They may grow deeper just when circumstances dictate separation. This is a ground grief grows in.

The Well-housed Homeless

Many of the recently-retired, often recently-widowed, land in delightful housing where they aren't at home. They may not have to cook, clean, check the furnace, or clean the gutters, but what involvement makes it home? If you don't want to cook, you still know what you think cooking should result in, and that isn't always what is offered you. It may be tasty, but the taste is strange. *De gustibus non disputandum est.*

Retirees who opt for this are well-housed, you might even say they are well-hotelled or well-resorted, but where is home? *What* is home, anyway? Certainly not four unfamiliar walls, closer together than you're used to, maybe more expensive to live in, but requiring of the tenant no self-investment. Home is shelter, but a great deal more than protection from rain and cold. The unseen shelter is most needful. "Home" is a matter of perception.

I've heard retirees refer to their comfortable, attractive living-places in terms of prison. "Come around to my cell and see me," one said. They are posh prisons, but prisons all the same. What, after all, is the definition of a jail? It is a place you can't get out of when you want to.

Transportation for medical care and minimal shopping is provided, but that is not the same as freedom to move around spontaneously. Necessary transport is all a retirement complex can practically offer.

However attractive, these places are not home, for home is never just a building. When you say "going home" you don't mean house, you mean place, in the broadest sense. You mean community, where living is laced with relationships of varying quality and depth, where every-day activities are carried on through streets and into buildings that contain your own history. It isn't just a place you know; it's a place where you are known.

The homelessness of old age is seldom a lack of physical shelter. It is the invisible need for community, for attachment, even for what might be called communion. This home-that-isn't-home distorts perceptions; the most important is self-perception.

These are well-housed homeless, these of the new generation, as well as the shoved-out-to-the-end oldest one. The senior seniors brag about their age, since they are finally pretty sure where they are. In general, physical location doesn't matter so much if you know where you are emotionally and spiritually.

That may be part of the problem of junior seniors: They are still uncertain whether or not they are "old," and, for them, "old" is still slur. They are not at home in their age category, whatever that is. (Nobody is *ever* "at home" in a category.)

These people are not at home in the building they sleep in, often not in the state they now vote in. They are not sure where they belong, and have no idea where they are going. That's a definition of "lost." They are no longer at home in their lives.

Homelessness is exile, occasion of yearning and grief, and if others think your sadness unreasonable, it can carry a sense of shame and go unexpressed, to burrow deep in the psyche, a pain nobody knows how to heal, most of all those who hurt.

Those who live in the streets are not the only homeless, as those who lack food are not the only hungry. A woman admired for her vitality, achievements, and involvement, surprised everybody when she was asked for a definition of old age and she answered: "a long grieving."

Collecting Losses

The old are particularly subject to the most personal and vital kind of loss, those part-losses of themselves and their world that we call sensory deficits. This is literally a matter of perception, since it is loss of the ability to perceive fully. It usually also alters the way its victims are perceived.

Sensory losses are not restricted to old age, but thought an automatic part of aging. Yet the middle-aged and small children have sensory lacks, deafness, blindness, lameness. In the young, it is thought tragic and exceptional, as it should be. In the old, it is accepted as "normal," but inability to hear or see clearly is *not* "normal" at any age, only more "usual" in the old.

Loss of sight is serious deprivation, and carries loss of independence. The loss may not be total, and there may be new ways of dealing with it, but even at best, it can be devastating.

Hearing loss may seem less threatening to the psyche, but its deprivations are only less visible. Where blindness imposes dependency, deafness imposes isolation. The perception lost is social, since it is chiefly through speech that we communicate. That loss can be a form of solitary confinement.

Even a partial hearing deficit affects personality by its distortion of language, damaging relationship for all concerned. I knew a woman who had been totally deaf for years, when her hearing was surgically restored. She told me how her distorted hearing led to paranoia and to final hospitalization. When I met her, she could hear well, and was emotionally whole. She had regained sanity, but not the years of shared humanity she'd lost.

We tend to trust what we see, and hear, and touch. When we can't hear clearly, we may believe distorted words. Even good hearing in old age can find the sound of consonants unclear, and it is primarily the consonants by which we differentiate words.

Many people who use corrective lenses to see better are not willing to use technical aids for good hearing. They may assume they hear well because they hear something, but when you have to guess, you risk misunderstanding. Pride can be bought too dearly.

I've taught many students with varying degrees of hearing impairment. Those who accepted the loss were aware they might not understand, and asked for repetition. Their hearing lack had little effect on class participation. A few denied their loss, and seemed to transfer their anger to the class. I was never sure how much they understood, since they wouldn't tell me, and this left great gaps in their benefit from the course.

When I used what I called my "Beethoven speech," it brought forth an "aha" from hearing-impaired students. It's really only a reference, when I say that a poem should, if possible, be listened to. I suggest, "If you are where you can't

36

read it aloud, read it silently, at the speed of speech, and *hear* it with the ears inside your head, the ears Beethoven had to use in composing his later works." This touched them in a remarkable way. It's useful.

All the things you ever heard are still stored in your mind. Maybe you can train your wonderful brain (with its untried capacities) to recall some of them more clearly. Maybe failing eyesight can similarly recover stored scenes, re-experience them. A lot of our remembering is only "remembering *that,*" data-retrieval, but there is also a kind of memory by which you are pulled back into an event.

Data-retrieval is a necessary intellectual feat. What I call remembering-into is *anamnesis* (literally "re-calling"), a bringing back. It is sensory, experiential. Computers do data-retrieval wonderfully; they can't experience. They can't see, hear, smell, touch, as the human mind can, when it remembers into the past.

Anamnesis, however factual, is closer to imagination than to information recall. Sensory remembering can even lead toward the deeper seeing we call insight, to vision in the greater sense, and to more complete hearing, the "taking in" that "comprehension" literally means. So much of what we think we hear only skims by our ears. Of course, that is all much of it deserves.

Physical sensory processes are close to emotional and spiritual senses of wonder, amazement, eagerness. It is these we use in gaining wisdom and in perceiving more deeply than the visible, and beyond it. It has long been believed that loss of one sense makes others sharper. Can my mind be trained to help that happen? Can my heart be part of the training? If it does happen, can we learn to do it better? Can the process apply to spiritual and emotional senses?

Sensory losses don't only affect a person's perception of his surroundings, they affect others' perception of him, and sometimes with good reason. Out of embarrassment or frustration, the partially-sighted may decline opportunities for relationship. The partially-hearing may either retreat from conversation, or else talk more, to avoid the problem of not hearing. This can be done unaware, but turn conversations into monologs, lose interaction.

The less obvious a loss, the more it may be misunderstood. A teacher has told me how children try to help a blind classmate but tend to think the hearing-impaired unintelligent. "Dumb" once meant only unable to speak.

Other sensory losses, often unnoticed, are more important than they seem. The loss of taste keeps people wondering why nobody can cook well any more. The perception is of change in food, but the change is mostly in the perceiving. Olfactory loss can be dangerous, since it lets perils hide. Sadly, it also makes the past less accessible, because besides being an "early warning system" for danger, odor-perception is a powerful emotional trigger and a memory stimulant.

Modern technology can replace some lost functions, not always perfectly but usually well enough to make a qualitative difference. Using these aids may take work, patience, and creative endeavor; sometimes using them is more of an art than a skill. But what that was worthwhile did we ever not have to work at? And what can be more worth effort and patience than any possible sensory gain? It is restoration of lost parts of ourselves. When such losses are only partial, *that does not make them trivial.*

When these losses are not presently replaceable, this calls for even greater creative encounter. That human losses require a creative response should not surprise us. The intricate inter-workings of the human organism in all its plenitude of powers do resemble a work of art more than that of natural laws, though even those have their hallmarks. In the diminishing of human powers, it is art we must develop, remembering that we have creative resources we are not aware of until we call on them.

Then there are others: loss of mobility, flexibility, energy, and self-determination. That last one is something whole peoples have been known to fight and die for.

Not all the old suffer the same losses, but each aging person likely is losing something. Many are, in effect, collecting losses, where they used to collect valuable or attractive objects, skills, knowledge, and experience. Collected losses are different. Being a collection makes objects more valuable; it makes losses more damaging. Every emotional loss affects others. They can add up to more than their sum, even to the felt loss of a future, loss of identity.

It is accumulated losses that can bring that "long grieving," can trigger depression that imitates illness, emotional instability, and dementia. The anxiety that roots in fear of loss is as emotionally damaging as any physical fear. The list of threatened losses is long. Heading it is loss of control, whether in forced conformity, lost autonomy, competence, mobility, dignity. The assumed automatic loss of memory gets more attention than it merits. Studies increasingly show no automatic memory loss due to the aging process. Apparently, the way memory works may change somewhat, but possibly as much for the better as for worse.

The list is long, but so is any list of possible gains: coping skills, ability to share and relate, daring to risk, self-knowledge. There are many more, these are among the most valuable. For some, there is a world gained. The gains are harder than losses to notice and describe. We are used to a benign world, surely a gain in itself, if you become aware of it.

Physical changes have more urgent metaphoric equals. Mental and emotional rigidity are more painful, more life-threatening, than arthritis. Vanishing eagerness and sense of purpose are more to be deplored than waning physical energy. Romance, intimacy, and affection are more important than sexual outlet, although, whatever past opinion held, sexuality is inherent in the human experience to the end of life. In old age, opportunity is more likely missing than desire. In humans, sex serves more purpose than continuing the race, and some must grow old to find that out. At the least (not confined to sexuality), people need touching and being touched, physically and emotionally. Many are alone in their lives, with human physical nearness unavailable.

Do we see old age as a "problem?" If we look for that, it is what we will see, just as youth is a "problem" to that angle of vision. No age has a corner on problems, else "mid-life crisis" would not be a cliché. Prophecies tend to be self-fulfilling. The importance of the greatest losses or gains is in how they are perceived, most urgently in how they make the subject perceive himself or herself. Self-perception, however, is largely directed by expectations—those of others and of oneself.

The Great Symbols

Mentioned earlier was the loss of freedom of movement, loss of the car. Noting serious depression in residents of a retirement facility, I kept finding that the severe trauma, the incurable wound, was a recurring and deadly combination of losses—of people, place, and car. I think the loss of the car was the biggest obstacle to adjustment, for it made many other adjustments impossible. Without transport, there is no finding of shared interests, no learning a new place. There is not even access to fellowship in worship, because you become part of a church community by what goes on during the week and after services, when the van from where you live has gone back there.

Volunteer work can be fulfilling for the displaced, and every city cries for volunteers to do its works of social service and humane concern, but the worker has to get to where the work is.

There seem to be a couple of basic freedoms seldom talked about. They are the freedom to move around and the freedom to choose relationships, to make meaningful connections. These are not only present needs; they are doors to the future. Their loss leaves a sense that there is no future worth looking toward.

Retirees who move to a new place find themselves being the proverbial "stranger in a strange land," and this is *two* problems.

All these things interconnect. Much of one's feeling of significance comes from connections that are now tentative at best, and from achievements unknown to one's present neighbors. How do you establish an identity in new acquaintanceships? The attempt may feel too boasting to be acceptable to you, or sound too boasting to be acceptable to others. Or both. If you are shy to begin with, that turns into retreat.

With no one around who knows you, gone is that vague but necessary feeling we call familiarity. Familiarity doesn't breed contempt; without some degree of it, there is alienation.

Collecting losses is more than a present matter. With the onset of trauma, old losses are felt anew, old wounds are opened. Speaking intellectually, the old have the advantage of having known these and recovered, having found "ways to cope," techniques of living. But this return of past fears and sufferings is not an intellectual matter. It is a re-experiencing. Old wounds hurt again, no matter how well they were once healed. It isn't coping mechanisms that are needed, but relief of pain, new healing.

I think churches have a responsibility here that has been little examined. The new parish knows nothing of your old pain, would be at a loss if it knew. If pain stayed past, it wouldn't matter, but it has been brought back into your life. Strangers wouldn't see it as relevant now, and "old wounds waking" may happen at a less than conscious level, but the retiree has little sense of "belonging" with fellow-worshipers. Anyway, the old "belongings" took a long time to develop, and there is little sense of either time or ability to make new ones.

There may be available transportation to worship, which is the *sine qua non* of the parish's existence, but that is not where personal relationships are forged. That is done in shared work, play, shared purpose. The newcomer may have done those elsewhere, but past involvement doesn't count if it wasn't done here.

Is the Church really only a series of local bodies? Is one's membership in the whole, in its vastness and depth, unrelated to the way a life gets lived and its needs filled? The Church has been talking about our nomadic culture for decades, but I don't think it has really done much adapting to and caring for the needs that arise from that. The deepest needs of the old are seldom visible, but I think the deepest needs in all ages are probably invisible, as horrendous as some visible ones are.

What is *not* needed here is obviously "charitable" action, so much as personal compassion that is concerned, brotherhood that relates, caring that sees and listens. Listens! That is a key. These things come from individuals, not from committees.

Americans are very good at meeting obvious needs, but these are difficult to discern or to address. They may be impossible to address, but the attempt merits creative concern and thought. In national Church and in parishes, they deserve work of the best minds and hearts. The churches must make the Church aware of needs they find; the Church must help in meeting those needs.

All social organizations need to give thought to their old members, especially as they wander. To have been active and known in a local chapter, then be unnoticed, feel unwanted, in a new place raises questions about the meaning of fellowship.

The Walking Wounded

All this talk of losses in old age sounds more one-sided than it is. There are gains and opportunities. Even when sight is dim, there may be insight usually impossible to those younger. Where there is little freedom to move around, there is more freedom to rest, enjoy what brings joy, and do it in tranquility.

There are expendables. The old are no longer responsible for what others, like family members, do, and it is good for them to remind themselves of that. Many things can be jettisoned, and the resulting freedom and lightness are wonderful.

You can give up competition, reserving only what is pleasant stimulus. You no longer need to measure everything, you no longer must keep up with the Joneses. Who knows where the Joneses are now? I remember well my delight when I realized I didn't have to have an opinion on everything. Even anything.

In old age, says modern research, except for effects of disease, one seldom loses mental ability (exception: disuse). Memory, they tell us, works very well, especially when you consider there is so much more material to work through. The proverbial "absent-minded professor" is not absent-minded because he is old but because he has more important things on his mind.

Along with losing things, the old gain things worth having: a sense of proportion, the daring to risk, self-knowledge, freedom to experience in new ways. Many are wounded by circumstance, but they are usually the walking wounded. They can heal.

From what I have seen, one of the chief gains of old age is the ability to laugh and to cry, and without shame for these evidences of humanity.

The most significant undertakings, and most rewarding when achieved, are the acceptance of what is, the knowledge of and respect for who you are, the honoring of the human.

"They are no longer at home in their lives."

THE RESIDENTS

We have less in common than you think,
more than sometimes is good for us,
and less than we probably need.

We are done with making a living
or feeding and bedding the one who did.
Now we must make a life, and nobody taught us how.

In school they taught us to count
but not to know what counts, what matters.
They taught us to read, gleaning facts,
but not how to stroll among words on a mountain
smelling their blossoms,
not how to roll in the grass of language
like a colt, or jump through hoops
of sound, skip the rainbow's rope.
They taught us to add and subtract, to keep
books, but not how to taste them.
We learned to record the whens and the wheres,
but not how to share what can't be recorded,
not how to dig in the depths in our hearts
using speech for a shovel.

We learned to fabricate yesterdays
and assume tomorrows
but not to converse at ease with today,
as a friend, listening for questions.

We worried some recognition out of a time
and a place, but these don't know us.
Like Bo Peep, we lost our importances
and don't know where to find them.

Since we weren't born here, this feels like exile
and we hadn't said our goodbyes.
Tied by a strand of place, we feel this a web,
vibrating; we sense, somewhere, the spider.

We've laid down burdens, our backs can't carry air.
We had gravity to fight. Now we're blasted from it.
The oxygen smells wrong, we can't tell up from down,
we suffer from weightlessness.

"Many of the old are alone in their lives. "

TRILITERAL*

The word, eleemosynary,
fits in file folders, boxed square,
neon-lighted, with automatic cover.
It is perceived by percentage.

Sun-lighted children in Mexico
held out dirty hands, pidiendo limosnas,
from the same root.
                    Alms
pervade the human world from penthouse
to dirt floor but uncover
as differently as cactus from euphorbia.

The hot, nourishing soup may steam
away the frigid air and still taste
colder than a Canadian jet stream.

The coin takes its temperature
from the immaculate hand that tosses it.
We all beg alms some time, wanting
the coin, or the hand.

*The 3-letter base of words for giving to human need is alike in English and Spanish. The combination of L, M, and S structures *alms, limosnas, eleemosynary.*

SIGNIFICANCE

The Invisibly Needy

We've learned that all humans have the same basic needs and that circumstances give us other ones that may differ. When infants, we must depend on others to fill our needs. As we mature, we increasingly fill them for ourselves. When we are old we return, some more, some less, to requiring that others provide them. But note that "more or less" and remember, too, that nobody can provide all basic needs, all the time. We are genetically social. Still, in general, old age finds people becoming less self-sufficient. To have been self-dependent and be so no longer feels like regression, deterioration. "Feels like." That feeling isn't always telling us the truth.

The basic hierarchy of human needs is for food, shelter, protection from harm. Then comes need for opportunity to develop physically, mentally, emotionally and spiritually. The physical needs are insistently visible; the deeper needs, less tangible, may be taken for granted. Yet some of these intangibles are so necessary that children can't thrive without them, yet the result of their lack may only become visible later.

The early needs don't vanish, but when mature persons are meeting them for themselves, we don't see them. If in old age the need for providers reappears, it can be mistaken for something else. When the old have food and shelter and protection, what about secondary needs? What about social needs?: the old are sometimes the invisibly needy.

Most human needs exist in balance: The need for security from fear is balanced by a need for challenge. The need for security is obvious, lack of challenge produces inertia as perilous as anxiety's tension. Our need to hide is matched by a need to reveal. Our need for a known past is paired with a need to look to the future. As social animal, the human needs the company of his kind, but he requires solitude, too.

Sometimes lack is covered up. The need for communication gets lost in mere noise. I suspect the common assumption that old age makes people repetitive may come largely from a sense that they weren't heard the first time—or the twentieth. Repetition is not restricted to the old, but expected then, so noticed. Have you ever really *listened* to the conversation of teen-agers? Or business men and women? Or scholars?

Some needs we can only fill for ourselves, beginning with a sense of humor, the presence of which can be a matter of life and death. It has nothing to do with jokes. Indeed, many jokes are disguised cruelty, and seniors usually know them for what they are. The person who laughs a lot may have no sense of humor. It depends on what he or she is laughing at. A sense of humor is mostly a sense of proportion, with a firm grasp on reality; this is also a part-definition of humility.

Humility is not abjectness, but the closest possible approach to objectivity. To be humble is to be a supreme realist regarding ourselves. Humility is not only a great virtue, it is a great life-enhancer, and has as little to do with self-derogation as a sense of humor has to do with jokes. Humility is a similar sense of proportion and firm grasp of reality, applied to oneself. No one can give you a sense of humor or the virtue of humility, at any age. We all, senior or youth, must get them for ourselves. It seems to be a bit easier in old age. Maybe this is why old age is supposed to be a time of wisdom, for humor and humility are its basic components.

What seniors always need from others are attention (being really seen and heard), respect, acceptance. And being wanted.

The Lying Cliché

That's *wanted*, not needed. The cliché about people needing to be needed is based on a misperception. Not only is it untrue, it's dangerous, but it has been accepted so long it is almost sacred. It has excused a great deal.

We all need other people in our lives, but often the compulsive need for one particular person can be a way of refusing the general need. Physical or other circumstances may create a need for help, but that's help, not a specific helper. children need those to care for them and love them, but that is a need for care and love.

Need for a person can hide a multitude of sins—on the part of needer and/or needed. To be "needed" is to be burdened by another, controlled by his lack, but it is also a way of being in control of the other. Such a "needed need" provides obligations that can be tools of manipulation, of control. On either side, or both. In human terms, control is power, and—tacit or overt—power does corrupt.

Deep in many an emotional relationship is imputed obligation: "I love you. Therefore you must . . ." or "If you really loved me you would . . ." These are instruments of control.

Under normal circumstances, I don't think any of us needs to be needed. What we do need is to be in community, even to be in communion with others, not all others but some others. Sometimes being needed feels like communion, and for some people it is the only way they know to have that. It is the way they were early programed to achieve happiness, perhaps to avoid rejection.

What I call being in communion comes from our social nature running true to form. It is probably in no two relationships the same, and any number can play. It is what, unrecognized, most people want, who may settle for togetherness, acceptance, needing or being needed. Good these may be, somewhere each falls short.

Shared work and shared pleasure create community. We need that, but it is shared purpose and shared vision that create communion, that fills emotional needs but goes deeper. It has a spiritual dimension, inexpressible, the deep sharing of what it is to be human. It eases the cosmic loneliness with which we are all born, and from which so many of us flee, by various paths, to similar disaster. We usually first know that loneliness vividly felt (if unlabeled) in adolescence, later to be hidden under layers of responsibility, busy-ness, under "being needed."

Loneliness Revisited

In old age, I think, that loneliness may again be vivid, yet unrecognized. An old person can want community or friendship badly but not know what is wanted. The lack may seem tied to the past because it is unidentified but hauntingly familiar.

Old age is supposed (mostly by writers who are not there yet) to be a time of tranquility and peace. What I have seen suggests that it's more often one of restlessness and unresolved conflict. The blame may be put on physical ailments, which can often explain almost anything, but often something deeper seems to be troubling.

Persons need to be honored, respected, for their value as human beings. Our society often teaches us we have to earn our worth. We don't. We are born with it; it is usually accorded to babies. All of us need freedom from excessive or unrealistic expectations of others, but we may try to live up to them in order to avoid the loneliness. More important, we all need freedom from our own excessive expectations, which are harder to recognize and harder to change. As humans, we try to earn the value we have, as artists try to earn fame.

Actually, healthy artists don't want fame so much as they want, even need, recognition, in the true sense, being known for who they are, and their art a part of that. The pull toward recognition is the desire to be truly known. We all need that recognition. The need for fame may come from a starved hunger for attention sometime denied. If fame does come, an artist is likely to find that it isn't the wanted reward, after all. Recognition was the right one. The drive toward fame is compulsion, kin to the need to be needed, not aspiration.

This is a difficult lesson, but when achieved, (and in old age it may be) it is strangely freeing. No longer does the possible Pulitzer get in the old writer's way. He can turn again to writing for (first, but not only) the joy and labor of the process, rather than more tangible rewards. The rewards are always most welcome, but are not a need.

Artists or not, seniors seriously need that freedom from expectations—their own expectations of themselves, the expectations others have of them, and the expectations they have of others. Expectations may be hidden, but a feeling of disappointment is the tell-tale rust that betrays their iron.

Seniors also need enough living-space to allow for the preservation of their individuality, and they need respect for it.

Essential Purpose

The biggest advantage an artist has is a sense of purpose, which is to aging mind and heart as essential as good exercise and diet are to an aging body. Even small purposes are not only life-enhancing but life-saving. Expectations push unremittingly and dangerously, purpose draws gently ahead.

Purpose is what gives you a reason for getting out of bed in the morning. No one can tell you what your purpose ought to be, but we do need to know it ourselves. We need time and attention to find it, even more, we need the desire. Like love, it is not contingent on approval, it needs no external justification.

It is a sense of purpose that matters. The aim itself may be long-buried or suddenly discovered. A purpose is rather like a goal, but more durable, more reachable, usually bigger, and open to exploration. A goal is somewhere you want to go, a place to be reached. A purpose comes from within, decision spurring action. A goal beckons from the future; purpose is right now, here.

Old age may be the time, for instance, to cultivate "the second art," undertaken as producer or as sensitive and knowing consumer. All arts need that kind of consumers. When the culture has those, it will have inspired and inspiring arts.

But the senior should not too quickly reject the idea of becoming an artist. Even for the beginner, the eagerness, the stimulation of creativity in action is the kind of "short-term stress" that scientists have found to be health-giving, to be the best way of release from the long-term stress (a very different thing) that can damage the body, whatever its age.

That old brain is still able to produce wonders. Findings of modern brain research reveal surprises. The old suppositions of continuing cell-deaths in the brain have been shown to be false. New nerve connections (by which mind-work is done) keep getting made, as long as the mind keeps receiving stimuli and being made to work.

Maybe you can't teach an old dog new tricks, but an old brain, except for specific disease processes, can teach itself new skills, new ways of creating, and can keep right on learning.*

Old people need acceptance and respect, but toleration is a subtle poison, to receiver and giver (if you can call it giving.) People are damaged by being tolerated. The only shield against it is compassion—not toleration—for those who devalue or fear what we are. That is hard work.

We have to fight for our dignity, for the continuing meaning of our lives, but the battlefield is not political. It is in ourselves, primarily, and in our relationships with others. It is in what we insist on, in what we permit—from ourselves first.

The Ultimate Loss

The ultimate loss occurring in old age is not the loss of friends and loved ones, as devastating as that is, nor the loss of wealth or beauty or status, but the loss of the sense of significance that any of these have given us.

Whether our lives are in fact significant is not important. It is the feeling of significance, the feeling that they matter, to someone, in some milieu, that sustains people. Feeling that they don't matter can plunge them into depression and despair.

The need to feel significant exists in a context. To look at the stars, to stand at the foot of a mountain, to read the thoughts and acts of great men and women, even to look at the unsolved

---

*The MacArthur Foundation, sponsor of research on successful aging, has published *The Mind,* by Restak. It is available on cassette for $29.95.

riddles of North American petroglyphs and the cave walls of Lascaux, is to know my own insignificance, and grow by the experience. But somewhere in my daily life, and not only in my past, I need an indication that my existence matters to somebody, to some persons or cause, in order for it to matter to me.

This is why retirement is so hazardous to the health of the "important" business man, why the loss of relationships is threatening to the well-being of the matriarch, why the loss of beauty can devastate the beauty. What made them feel they mattered? What was their treasure? There were their hearts also.

When that treasure is gone, men and women are in a real sense disheartened. What is lost was the core of their being. So many treasures are vulnerable to time.

You see, it really isn't that people "need to be needed," but that they need to know they matter, that they matter now. That knowledge can't be gotten from mere verbal assurance.

Life has never offered any guarantees about anything. The past may look solid by hindsight, but it was not so certain when we were proceeding by trial and error (it is the only way life is lived). If we don't remember the insecurities and dead ends, the losses, the disappointments, it is because our memories have become so selective that the potholes and quicksands and deserts of youth and middle life look as green now as the grass on the other side of any fence. We have climbed over the fence of old age without noticing, and fallen onto that other side.

Significance and importance are not the same thing. One can be "important" (in terms of society's values) and not be significant; a remarkably significant person can be totally unnoticed by society. It's a question of ultimate values, not the ones we persuade ourselves consciously to put first, but those we really, in our inner being, consider vital. Those are our real values, it is those by which we will measure our significance.

Sometimes our suffering, even victimization, is the price we are willing to pay for a feeling of significance. Lacking a feeling they are significant, some of the old will lose the present moment, if they no longer live in it. They may have gone totally back to the past, in what is not so much a retreat as a rout, or they may exist tentatively and fearfully in a future possibility of disaster.

Our sense of identity is a way we experience what we see as significance; a sense of significance, though tentatively gained, is knowing who and what we are. The opposite of "significant" is "trivial," and trivial things can entertain, briefly, but a life spent in gossip and small talk is a life never quite experienced.

The most important losses are not physical. If seniors are surrounded only by strangers who don't know their history, their achievements, their values, their importances, then they have lost the basics—roots, loves, freedom, significance.

The Child Out of Hiding

If we no longer say much about deficits accompanying old age, it may be for no better reason than that "nice words are easier to swallow." We stop using the real words for things that bother us and substitute euphemisms, thinking that changing what we call a thing will change its nature. It's a try at verbal magic, as old as speech. In northern Europe long ago, people were afraid of the words ("runes") on gravestones. They thought words so associated with death were magic.

In the hands of a magician, words do work a kind of magic, but not quite the way the ancients thought. Now magicians of words are authors or politicians. Long ago in southern Europe, "rhetoric" was the most important study, that of using language to persuade. One thing it taught was to use nice words for things you wanted people to like and nasty ones for what you wanted them to dislike. It is still going on, and will.

Euphemisms only work for a while. When they really say what they substituted for, the real word disappears. Then we have to find euphemisms for the euphemisms.

To talk about unpleasant reality nowadays, we use scientific terms. Science is our current magic. We don't say now that demented people are in their second childhood, but they suffer cerebral dysfunction, or they are cognitively impaired. It still happens, although better knowledge of the way brains work reveals that it's seldom caused just by the age of the brain's owner.

The idea of "second childhood" does merit thought, however. We know the human brain does much of its developing in response to stimulus, beginning in the womb, a place not nearly so well insulated as we used to think. The developing brain makes new synapses (nerve connections) in response to stimulus. Familiar things have a role to play in learning, but so do unfamiliar things that require new adaptations, i.e., new synapses.

As a child grows, its mental processes become more complex, and more hidden. Maybe in old age, if life becomes less complex, the child is more visible.

That is life, not brain processes, becoming simpler, and I don't mean that life becomes easier. Usually not so much is going on and life is less mixed up. The bushes of business and busy-ness are being pruned, which may or may not be welcomed. It does have to be adapted to.

The child the old person still is (it has been the same baby/child/adult all along) begins to come out from behind those adult bushes, if it seems safe to. This is not return, not a second childhood; it's a continuous child come out of hiding.

The most mature, responsible adults can seem "childish" when sick. This is probably not a regression but a clearing, necessary to health. The world and our parents want us to grow up, but minds and bodies and spirits may need for us to be whole. In old age, the game of hide-and-seek is over.

If so, then what the healthy old one needs is what was needed in childhood: not just toys to play with but stimulus to respond to. Any child can tell you that too many toys is confusing, easy games are soon boring, hard lessons are more fun than busy-work.

Not long ago, I was teaching seniors how to write their memoirs. Once we dispensed with the idea of mere chronological reporting, we had a good time writing history (personal history, of course, but all well-written history is personal). The students were learning to remember on purpose, to remember-into their lives as children.

One student wrote pages of detailed exposition of what she thought she should be writing about, but she didn't like the way it came out, and neither did I.

When we discussed it, she said the really wonderful memories were not the famous relatives and the parties she went to with her sisters but the hard days and nights of helping her farmer-father with the animals. She spoke of getting up during the night to check on the ewes, going into the barn carrying a lantern in the freezing dark, to stand there in the quiet bitter cold "hearing the animals breathing."

Physically, it had been hardship, but it was the childhood she had chosen, been allowed to choose, and enjoyed all her life. It was hard, it was work, it earned her college tuition (her parents said she had "saved the cost of a hired man") and those years and her college ones gave her a joy her sisters never knew. She thought it wasn't what people wrote memoirs about.

I told her it was exactly what she had to write memoirs about, and she was off into the writing, full speed ahead. It was the stuff of human reality, the account of a real relationship, lived quietly and at depth, with the father she worked alongside.

I've been listening, and the things people remember best are often not the "good times" but the significant ones, times when a child was allowed into important areas of the grown-up world, by tragedy or responsibility or choice. It was "when our house burned down," and "when my brother's wife died, and I was the only one with him," and "when I was allowed to go to my aunt's and she let me eat all I wanted to," and "when I was old enough to help with the little ones—so I am still very good with babies."

So many of the things we remember as important are not so much happy times or sad ones, but those events that made life worthwhile, that made us aware of our own significance. It was that way in childhood; it still is. Maybe one of the chief sources of distress in today's old age is that there is so little happening that is worth remembering. We bog down in trivia.

"In old age, the game of hide-and-seek is over."

DIRECTION

"Without knowledge of the past, the way into the thickets of the future is desperate and unclear."

Loren Eiseley, *The Unexpected Universe*

We no longer hear how we survived this far,
or plan survival. We parody the future,
as if it were fiction, but the possible
is the unexpected, not to be armored against.

Without roots, how do I hold onto earth
in winter winds? Without knowing where I come from
how do I know where I go? Peace must root
in my groping mind, more than half hidden.

I don't know what hides there, as I don't know
the hearts that held each other long enough
to make my unexplained existence. I know
only the crust of that linking and breaking.

I probed for explanations in what was
beyond explaining. I must leave cool reason.
I must go to the child I was, I am, and hear
through those ears, magic of loved language.

Smells told me what I couldn't see, I heard
what I should have been deaf to, stumbled over
my mother's perfume, and in the night, jasmine
falling to cobblestones. Music pierces my shell.

Knowledge entered through exploring fingers,
silent eyes. I had to touch to believe.
Now I go touching into old rooms, smell
their silence, stroke the empty walls.

A small hand pushes through thickets
rustling with life, sending strange odors,
where leaves shine and shadows are painted.
When the way grows desperate and unclear,
I can go through, using a child's tools.

"A sense of purpose . . . is to aging mind and heart as essential as . . . exercise and diet are to an aging body."

EVENTS

*Events tend to clot, like blood, sending
tender filaments to snag on one another
weaving a net of protein, time-toughened,
a web to trap hopes and regrets,
fears, questions. Sometimes
they turn into scars.*

*Is this what I have gained those wounds
preparing for? How can it be? I am still
preparing, still working things out, finding
no one right way. There may be no
wrong one. I have but a learner's
permit for my life.*

THE EDGE OF THE WATER

We come down into the water, and try to say how it feels. I didn't even know my toes were damp, but here I am, wading in it. This ebb tide shallows the water, revealing things hidden on the sea-floor. Wading is not adventure, but it takes effort. "Tide" is a word for change, but the verbal mate of "ebb" is "flood." They remind us of the living pulse of ocean, the world, and ourselves. The water recedes, but that pulse continues.

CULTURAL INFECTIONS

You Can't Get Away from It

No culture ever provided all that human beings require for total good health. All cultures have their weaknesses, even what might be called infections, which trouble human beings and their relationships. Some cultures are better than others, though that depends much on the viewpoint of judgment, but no culture is totally wholesome. Eden can't come again, and anyway Adam didn't like it well enough to stay. We probably wouldn't either. Literature tells us that utopias are not all they claim to be, since most of the well-known accounts were written as satire.

You can't get away from culture — you inhale it, you walk around in it. It's a climate.

Even the rooms in retirement housing are pervaded by the culture they inhabit. You may be somewhat set apart, people who have lived in and survived earlier versions, but that doesn't inoculate you against the infections of the present one. Even if the "good old days" were really that good (which is moot) where you live is here and now.

It isn't just that the currents of our culture drive our thinking and our actions, but that our very spirits are hostages to the *zeitgeist,* the "spirit of the age." These infections take away human options. They set up for us goals that we head for instead of trying to reach our own.

Competing with Whom?

We've mentioned competition, which belongs in the business district, and under some restrictions even there, but in this culture gets taken home. Competition isn't always pathologic, but when it is, it is deadly to all that is humane.

Competition is so general that it "feels" normal, and it's hard to know when you are being plagued by it. When I teach creative writing I have a few house rules, and the first of these is that competing isn't allowed. Yet again and again, students reading their work begin by comparing it to what has been read before. They say, "that's a hard act to follow," or make some derogatory remark about what they are preparing to read.

Really listen to conversations and you will hear constantly the language of such value-comparison, overt or disguised. What is important is recognizing it in yourself. It's almost incurable in modern America, but at least try to control the fever of it. How? Think of the difference between a jockey with a race to be won and a horseman riding in the park. Which do you feel like, most of the time? This life is not a race. The track isn't oval (if it does sometimes feel like you're going in circles), nobody is betting money on you, and there is no finish line to cross before somebody else does. When you feel tense and badgered, ask yourself if anybody declared this a contest.

If it isn't a race, then we are free to sit loose in the saddle and watch what's around us, free to roam through the woods, free to go where we are led by better things than prizes.

If this is a competition, we must always be adult, our attention riveted on someone else's achievements. But we are not only these stressed grown-ups; we are still the children we always were. If it isn't a contest, the child can come out and play.

What Price Independence?

Related to competitiveness, but less obviously an infection, is compulsive independence. Independence seems so rightly admirable, and so innate. It is rather dependence that we think of as pathologic. Like a lot of other things, this is a matter of degree and of circumstances. In old age, it is independence (splendid as it is) that is most likely to develop complications. But it is always a relative matter. Like a lot of other things, its pathology lies in degree.

The first step in the cure of compulsive independence lies

in the honesty to admit that no one of us, however competent, could possibly live totally on his or her own. That's one reason why human society of some kind is necessary. A little attention to what our lives require from others helps alleviate the symptoms, and raises one's humility index in the process.

Humility? Me? It's funny how human beings always think of humility as a virtue in others, but want no part of it themselves. Yet those who have achieved it are evidence that it's a great pain-reliever, among other desirabilities. Those who claim to have achieved it usually don't know much about it. Basically, humility is being willing to share the human condition, refusing to aspire to divinity.

Illogical as it is, along with the compulsion to independence in this culture, there exists a surprising fear of loneliness, which people confuse with being alone. Many men and women marry primarily to escape being alone, and many of those marriages don't last because one or both of those involved want to keep the independence while they fend off the aloneness, a classic example of the attempt to eat your cake and have it. Some degree of dependence is the price of relationship close enough to hold loneliness at bay, and aloneness, even sometimes loneliness, can be the price of independence.

It isn't just that we don't want to be by ourselves in the world. We want someone to love us, we want to feel that we are, to somebody, the most important person around.

It seems to me that often loneliness is not so much wanting someone to be loved by as wanting someone to love. There need to be receivers for love, willing to accept the love that's offered, not demanding one tailored to specifications. Maybe this is why animals and small children are so delightful to the old, because they respond to love as given.

We need to love, and we need to get response. This need for reciprocity is felt even in the giving of gifts. When a present is unacknowledged, there is a feeling akin to outrage at being taken for granted. It isn't formal thanks that are necessary, but response. It's not a matter of manners, but of humanity.

I treasure the remembrance of, for instance, a valentine mug I gave Edward, because I recall his insistence that it best kept the coffee hot. It didn't, of course; the warmth was of a different kind.

Loneliness is one of the kindred ills of depression, but not the same thing, and it has little to do with being alone. You can be more lonely in a crowd than by yourself. All those people around you can seem like walls.

Solitude is a blessing, often a healing balm, and certainly a necessity, at least occasionally. Loneliness is a very different matter, but people will run away from solitude because it means being alone. And they will avoid those who are alone, apparently thinking it may be catching.

In the company of seniors, you will find that old couples and old singles, in the same place, do not a community make. The singles congregate, loosely or compulsively, while the couples walk two by two, maybe toward some kind of ark. What happens when couples become singles, as they almost inevitably do? Terrible loneliness, for one thing. Along with grief, the survivor often drifts around miserably, not belonging with anybody else. Is this because of our culture's fear of aloneness, of solitude, and of possibly catching it?

In important ways, each of us is solitary. You must do your own searching, your own finding, your own experiencing, and your own intending. You must do your own loving. But you do these things in a world of almost infinite variety, of texture, of intensity—a world rich with life, whatever that is. You are given the planet and the stars for your home, and whether you understand what the gift is or not, you are given a life to be lived. The life has long been lived, but while it is still life, it is also yet to be lived, the same kind of life as your fellows are given. It requires both solitude and sharing.

Even if much of the life has already been lived, while it is still life, it is still a gift. The best thanks for a gift is to use it, and share that using as you can.

The Toxin of Perfection

My second house rule for students is that I forbid, in work or discussion, use of the word, "perfect," except in two technical contexts. Botanically, a perfect flower is one that has both male and female parts. Grammatically, the perfect tense of a verb refers to action that has taken place and is not continuing. Perfect means complete or completed, not flawlessness.

The search for perfection, in self or others, is following a will-o-the-wisp that leads to disaster. (It certainly stultifies experiment and exploration). Perfectionism is a deadly and pervasive infection. For what is alive and changing, like human beings, the word, "perfect," has no real meaning (also, like "unique," it is an absolute and has no degrees). Against what standard could it be measured?

Yet human differences are called imperfections, by parents, spouses, friends, teachers. How much self-devaluation comes from not being "perfect" by somebody's definition—worst, by your own?

I sometimes find seniors who will not let those closest to them, usually their children, know anything is wrong, physically or emotionally. This denial of vulnerability may come from a need to be seen as perfect. Unfortunately, it can as well come from a (possibly well-founded) mistrust.

Beware those who call themselves perfectionists. They are not people who look for perfection but ones who compulsively search for flaws, "imperfections." (They are always successful.)

The Common Cold of Civilization

There are a number of what might be called minor illnesses, the common colds of a culture. Like the real common cold, they have many causes, and can turn into something nastier.

There is our short-term thinking. We want short-term gains, even at risk of long-term losses. This now-ailing planet we live on is evidence of this. Ours are such short lives in cosmic terms that only lately have we begun to see that what happens day after tomorrow may turn out to be terribly serious. Short-term thinking also sends us into fits of panic over what we ought to know we can probably ride out.

Another name for this is the old "impatience." Our by-word is frequently "I want it now," so we avoid beginning actions that could bring us pleasure or value, if they will take time in doing it. This culture is certainly not lazy when it comes to most definitions of the word, but the work of thinking-through and of feeling-through gets short shrift.

There is another kind of impatience that makes havoc. This is the apparent necessity to keep moving, inability to sit still, to wait, to listen, to let things happen or fail to happen. We say, "Don't just stand there; do something," but sometimes what is needed is precisely that we stand there, and carefully do nothing.

This is why we fail to give friends in trouble what they may need most. We are so anxious to do something about their pain or trouble, even their grief, that we cut them short, shut them up, give them solutions when we don't even understand the problem. Usually what they need is our standing there, only listening.

Then there is our tendency to fragment everything.

With advances in medical knowledge and techniques, it became harder for any one physician to know all he needed to, so medical specialties developed, and now there is a strong temptation for a doctor to see the organ or system of his specialty rather than the patient as an interacting organism, the patient as person. Fortunately, this trend seems to be reversing, but it is only an extreme example of the over-all sectioning of matters, thinking in compartments, judging by parts. This not only leads to a lot of false judgments and missed diagnoses (medical or other) but it restricts the whole culture to superficiality.

It also leads to breaking up the population itself, creating unnecessary gaps and dissonances. It makes us think of real live people only as types of our mental categories, and then project onto persons qualities we've assigned to the categories. This produces, among other things, some self-fulfilling prophecies.

Seniors are often victims of this tendency, but they seem to do the fragmenting as much as anybody else.

It is frequently assumed that the old will be boring to the young (maybe because the middle-aged are) and that the young will frighten the old, since they seem to frighten middle-aged parents.

The "generation gap" is a rift between parents and off-spring, who seem to live in different cultures. There possibly could be bridges between adolescence and old age if the ends of the space to be spanned weren't set in different worlds. Like adolescents, who must cope with conflicting emotions and rapid changes in bodies no longer familiar, the old lose the security of the known, even in their own bodies. It may be that seniors could best understand teenagers, and teenagers best understand seniors, if they ever became sufficiently acquainted.

A fragmented people lives in jeopardy, so we need to do a better job of thinking whole.

On the other hand, we also lump. That's only another aspect of our categorizing. Thinking in categories, useful for scientists, is dangerous, sometimes vicious, in the laity. It's part of the all-or-nothing mental cop-out, the sensory sloth that doesn't want to bother to look around, to take in new information, and the pride that doesn't want to admit it was wrong.

The superficiality affects everything. Given the capacity for thinking and feeling deeply, we stay shallow. This explains the silliness of the "Don't worry; be happy" slogan which, in a world of crime and pain, of violence and need, loss and fear, is an affront to our own humanity, even said as a joke.

Sometimes the fear of being alone leads to compulsive membership, of various kinds. If the involvement is a way of sharing concern and labor, or a sharing of interests, it's a wholesome thing. I wish our organizations were more accepting of those who want to be part of them but who can't afford much cost of effort. An organization must have workers, but not everybody is able to do that work. Each member has his own limitations and commitments. I know seniors who no longer take part in affairs they would like to, because they can no longer "do their share." Who says what is anyone's share? Must it be all or nothing?

All-or-nothing is another of our common colds, along with the either/or cough.

In real life, very few things are heroic enough to wear white hats and few villainous enough to wear black ones. Mostly the context determines what is "good" and "bad." We find a lot of useful "maybes" and a real need for a some-time "sometimes." The either/or frame of mind tends to produce knee-jerk absolutes and instantaneous judgments.

Few things really fit the either/or. The world is set more in the mode of both/and, neither/nor, all-of-the-above, and what else? It is either/or thinking and all-or-nothing seeing that bring about the Slope Syndrome, in old age.

The Slope Syndrome

This culture tends to think of human ability only in terms of "can do" and "can't." Most seniors are at neither end of that scale. There is what I call the "Slope Syndrome" which might be defined as "can do but . . ."

The person who can put in a good half-day's work at the computer, or housework, or wielding a shovel for that matter, can't necessarily do it for a full day either comfortably or without damage.

Occasional short-term stress is stimulating, beneficial, but that same tension held too long can be harmful. Fatigue varies, in kind as well as amount. Work-tired is not the same as worry-tired, and neither is necessarily exhaustion.

What happens to seniors is a gradual wearing-down of physical capacity, loss (slight to major) of resilience, and diminishment of the ability to respond quickly to demand. We tire more suddenly, often more deeply, and we don't recover as quickly or as well as we used to. This doesn't mean we can't or shouldn't strain or work or play hard. It means we have to learn our limits, and keep learning them as they change.

The time and intensity of an activity are factors to consider. It's usually a matter of how much? and how long? and how vigorously? If we feel we need to stop, but don't show it, we hate to admit it, and we usually don't.

It's cumulative stress that should be taken account of, whether physical, mental, emotional or spiritual. I think of a friend with a year-old hip replacement. She can climb stairs a few times in a day without pain or harm. One more flight of stairs can set off pain that lasts for days.

Being over the hill means you aren't at the top of it but it doesn't say how far down, yet where you are makes a difference. To make it more interesting, you don't stay put. Where you are today is only slightly relevant to where you will be next week.

The ability to accomplish what you want to and to be socially active may just be the result of having found one's physical limits and learned to pace oneself. A seventy-five-year-old I know who still is self-employed found jury duty painfully fatiguing, long past the trial. She said, "I could handle it fine if they'd let me take a couple of rest periods."

Another senior in her seventies tells me of pain she earns if she doesn't stop when she knows she needs to. They are both over the hill. Neither is near the bottom, yet. Pushing past limits (and work doesn't have to be physical to be work) can be costly bravado, while within limits much is possible and enjoyable.

In old age, it is more the rule than the exception that there is lessened energy without severe disability. But in our world, it's all or nothing, rather, it's nothing or all. Most seniors are somewhere on the slope. Where they are says what they can do with comfort and safety and what will cost them pain and risk. Diminished energy, even disability, doesn't make you into a different person. Disability doesn't apply to all your one-time abilities. You can be more whole than ever before, in ways that can't be quantified, but less able in others.

Going downhill is not all bad. If you do it on skis or a sled, well, that's what you did all that climbing for. (Don't push this analogy too far—life offers few chair-lifts.) But even on skis, it takes skill and judgment if it is to give pleasure. I think the same may be true of "going down hill" in old age.

A Sign of Health

One strong evidence of health in this culture is the existence of "support groups," those sharing programs, usually based on AA's "twelve steps," meant to help people deal with self-destructive compulsions. While the proliferation of these programs may look as if we had a lot of people with severe problems (and we do, but we always have) I don't think this phenomenon speaks so much of a great increase in the compulsive disorders as it does to the healthy tendency of human beings to find ways of getting what they need, when it is lacking. People need community, and it is in such short supply now. These groups furnish it, along with much else.

Besides dealing with shared problems, these groups bring people together in a way that lets them relate in intimacy and trust. Since the support of extended family and/or neighborhood has eroded away, these groups supply what those once did. They are ways to health for the emotionally impaired, but also I've known people who simply found them humanly needful. In an impersonal world, they are gateways to fellowship.

Was the local church once a support system, while now it's a social obligation? A few decades ago, a teaching in mainline churches said: "The church exists for those outside."

A woman going through severe personal trauma said to me that if she wanted help from her church, by that logic she'd have to resign her membership. Social action of various kinds was where the churches' energy was being spent in those days, sometimes at the expense of its own members. Here was a classic example of either/or going off the deep end.

There are always needs inside any social structure. Loyalty and caring and compassion are owed to those who are close as well as those who are far off. Seniors are but some of the many individuals whose needs should concern fellowships they belong to.

The primary purpose of the church is the worship—the *shared* worship—of God. The betterment of men and women, fellowship, and any saintliness come from that. Alan Paton, who certainly put his beliefs into action where it was costly to do so, has drawn attention to this. But it is an intricately fashioned web of inclusions, not a need to choose between exclusive options.

Humans, as social beings, need communication. There is no relationship without it. For all our communication technology, we are shamefully poor at doing it close by.

What is needed, I am afraid, is not a different attitude to the needs of old age so much as a different attitude to what are human needs. The problems are universal, the results manifest in youth, in middle age (read: crisis), anywhere you look, if you are willing to see.

"you are given a life to be lived"

A DWELLING ON POSTULATES OF THE SCIENCE OF PLATE TECTONICS

My mother's world, to her
steadfast, as to Descartes and Aristophanes,
to Paul and Lear. The ground
was grounded under their wandering
feet, however their knees might shake.
They dared treacherous seas,
secure that rock was solid.

I learned too young the terrible news
Othello heard, that innocence
can be false, that the heart of the world
is inconstant. There is no rock
that does not flow or bend or buckle.
This was the end of innocence
whose other name is trust. Now babies
are born to knowledge of their birthplace
as a wicker basket bobbing
upon waves, to knowledge of planets pulling
the very planet, whether or not they pull
destinies. Well, why not? Why not wrench
grey tender matter almost jelly if they twitch
surging stone, melted to glowing ocean
far under us—not far enough.

Our mother earth is fire, wearing
a mummer's mask, offering magma
for milk. The air is rock. The waters
are more stable than mountains, fire
underlies, striving upward.

Our fathers dared uncharted oceans, we
uncharted continents, changing
like a waterspout. There are winds
under us. Innocence
must look inward.

Science hasn't made much difference in people, besides increasing their life-expectancy, but it has made a difference in how their world feels.

"our . . . spirits are hostages to the zeitgeist, *the spirit of the age"*

ANOTHER WILDERNESS

*This is a frontier
where battles must be fought
again, or fought at last.
No Waterloos, these,
the big wars are elsewhere.*

*Guerrilla actions
sudden from ambush
are launched by unknown enemies
and those forgotten
or assumed slain.*

*They appear from the woods
with arrows, hatchets,
or in familiar streets
with handguns, small rockets,
bombs, ordinary rocks.*

*They are seldom deadly
but they make it hard to clear
the brush, to move boulders,
build houses, plow these hard fields,
to reap grain for our hunger.*

REGRETS, REVISIONS, AND RENEWALS

Inverted Relationships

Time does some strange things to relationships. Tentative ones strengthen into pillars that can hold up the falling heavens and sturdy ones can fall down when nobody pushes them. I think the only thing you can be sure of is that Heraclitus was right. However things are, they won't stay that way.

Even with your children, as we have said, strange changes take place and sometimes those relationships become lop-sided, and hard to deal with. Anxiety about becoming a burden to descendants is one of the major worries of a lot of seniors; how to provide what seniors need is a many-faceted worry for a lot of juniors. Misunderstanding gets engendered either way. It seems there are about as many steps in the dance of the generations as there are dancers. It's no wonder feet get stepped on.

I have heard a good many seniors wondering how to keep their progeny from trying to run their lives, when they're still capable of doing it for themselves, and finally have the time to devote to it. I would say, only as a rule of thumb, that help is one thing; managing is another. If your CPA daughter offers to help you balance your checkbook, let her, and say "thank you" politely. If she tells you how to spend your money, say, "No, thank you." As often and loudly as necessary.

Part of the ground for problems is that grown children tend to be as sure they know it all as you were when you were their mother. Children also tend to want to make their own mistakes, the way you did, while the only experience you want them to learn from is yours. Further, they can't really know you as the person you are now, because the parent they think they remember gets in the way. The child you think you remember keeps getting in the way of your knowing them. You may be close (I hope you are) and you may love each other dearly (I hope you do), but even the love of family members can be as blind as Cupid is portrayed.

The problem isn't just the doomed role-reversal we mentioned earlier. You aren't likely to speak the same language, or if you do, you do it in different dialects, and this can lead to breakdowns in communication, overt or hidden. The overt ones are probably the least hurtful to everybody.

Time Runs One Way

Time runs one way, and if you try to reverse that, the result is likely to be contact that is head-on and dangerous. If you have to depend on your children physically or financially, that may be unfortunate but it can be lived with, sometimes gracefully. Rarely should you try to depend on them emotionally. They have their own inner worlds, and you have yours, and each is an alien if he tries to invade.

Time's mulishness about going in one direction gets mixed up in our regrets. All regrets should have expiration dates, like milk cartons. We should try to undo our damages just so long, then leave them for time and the grace of God to handle.

Time does take care of a surprising number of things, if we let it. The earth renews itself again and again, and so can we, the brothers and sisters of earth who have so often offended her.

(Her versatility shouldn't lead us to assume her survival of everything we can do.) Time brings renewal but note that the core of that word is *new*. Time cannot restore old wonders (there will be no more passenger pigeons) but it can sometimes make them into new ones. This can be done even to relationships, if the old status is not calcified.

Regrets are not the same as repentance. You regret actions which hurt others, showed you in a bad light, lost you money or prestige or self-respect. You regret hasty words and boneheaded judgments, lost opportunities, misunderstandings, bad choices.

The only things you repent of are sins, and repentance means something more than, and different from, regret. It means renewal, seeing new. It means thinking in new ways, a new way of *being*. It means change, which we'll deal with in the chapter after the next one. Repentance is never easy.

On Receiving and Giving

Old age is a time of increased dependence, and for most Americans, this is one of its more horrid possibilities. It is something we regret even before it happens, because we see being dependent as a slur on character rather than a challenge to it.

Public figures often assert (with more flippancy than wisdom) that they "don't intend to grow old gracefully." They forget their only alternative (besides dying young) is to grow old awkwardly. "Gracefully" in the old phrase refers to humility, generosity, and balance, not a dancing body, social "niceness," or good looks.

Some time ago, Anne Morrow Lindbergh, in a TV interview, said she hoped in old age to find a place where she "might give." The idea is hardly new, and is a proper thing to say at retirement. What is *not* said is that there may come a time when you have nothing to give, at least nothing that takes energy or independent action. Or maybe there are no receivers around. Givers have to have receivers. There are many old men and women who feel that no one wants what they have to give. I'm reminded of Florida Scott-Maxwell's comment in her journal that one of the frustrations of old age is that you have things to say and nobody wants to hear them.

There are many who would echo that pious wish to keep giving, but not all who grow old will be able to do it. Some will need to acquire the grace of receiving, and in this culture that seems to be a lost art.

Art it is. I think we might well take note of the element of pride, along with the graciousness, in the desire to remain a giver. This society doesn't know how to accept. Who stops to think that such ignorance is hard on others who must do the giving, on the givers who must live with a churlish and grudging gratitude in the unwilling dependents?

I learned this in watching my mother-in-law, who, as she became more dependent, became increasingly delightful to be around. After she was confined to an infirmary bed, all the attendants spent their free time with her, enjoying her talk, her wit and warmth. Her kind of giving made theirs a joy.

There have to be those who care for the dependent; any who can make the job more pleasant, more rewarding, more humane, are just as altruistic as those who give in order to feel their own worth. It may not be said, but the message we usually get is that giving is not only more blessed but more admirable than receiving. It's not quite that simple.

"I've given," said one senior I know, "and it doesn't seem to have made any difference to anybody." It probably did make a difference, but nobody let him know it.

One would think this might be a place where seniors could give to one another, but the prevailing attitude of the old to the old seems to be little different from that of anyone else.

The trouble is that in this culture we don't learn that you are born with a right to exist, that you don't need to earn it. We claim to believe in the dignity and value of the individual, regardless of his or her "contributions," but our world all too often acts otherwise. That may be what we think; it is apparently not what we feel.

We grant that importance to babies, who don't "contribute," but is that because there is in them potential for contribution? because they are charming, in a culture where appearance is so often taken for personality or character? When there is no potential for visible productiveness, what then? Oh, we say the elderly are important for themselves, and their past service is appreciated, but this is a "now" world, and the message in action is mostly, "What have you done for me lately?" It is tragic when it is the senior himself, herself, who is asking the question.

No wonder depression is endemic among the old, especially since the depressed often feel guilty about being depressed. They are shunned, so while people become depressed because they are lonely, they are often lonely because they are depressed.

Love in the First Grade

Because lately there has been popular development of a mode of philosophy and therapy that includes emphasis on building self-esteem in adults or children, this has come to be called the "me generation" by some who would insist on total concern with the needs (and wants) of others. This is another either/or trap.

To "be good to oneself" is not necessarily to be selfish, self-centered, or oblivious to others. The biblical injunction is to "love one's neighbor as oneself" not "instead of oneself," which is the way it has too much been taken. It was first addressed to an audience of people who did know how to love themselves. In this case, the both/and is explicit in the injunction, as well as in the fact that human beings normally begin life by loving themselves and demanding their needs.

A patient said, in tears, to her psychiatrist, "The problem is that he *does* love me *exactly* the way he loves himself, and it is going to be fatal to both of us."

Love begins at home, and when it does so in health it doesn't stop there, for that is not the nature of love. Love learns its arts and its limits, its purposes and its directions, very soon and very close, beginning with the child's self and soon embracing those close by. Self is where love's first grade class meets. If we fail the lessons there, we do our loving poorly ever after, whether it is loving ourselves or our neighbors. In our nineties, we love as we learned it in the nursery.

Generosity is one of the most winsome of the virtues, and it, too, should not exclude the giver. I know so many seniors who find it difficult to be generous to themselves, who can buy gifts for others who don't need them while they do without things that could make their own lives more comfortable, or even more enjoyable. Generosity is more than giving gifts, or even giving alms. It is the open-ness that doesn't feel driven to judge (self or others), it's the sharing of whatever is delight-making. Remember that to *share* is to partake as well as to offer.

Being generous to oneself is a good way to practice doing it well, for the sake of everybody in your life.

Sins and Non-sins

Human sinfulness exhibits very little originality, but temptations vary by circumstances, and old age is one of them.

The old "seven deadlies" are subject to some misleading interpretations, and sometimes overlap rather confusingly. Some sins are more compelling in one age than another, if you interpret rigidly, which I am not going to.

Take what is called gluttony. Does that mean falling off your diet too often, or does it have a deeper sense? I think this sin, whose every-day name is "greed," reaches much further than the dinner table or the candy-box. Surely it means the refusal to give up what has been enough, it means to keep wanting more. That's not just bad manners. Many seniors are pretty ungracious about giving up things when they've had their share of them. Take youth, for example.

If this refusal is tied to a compulsive concentration on what is possessed by someone else, it is envy. Maybe we envy the young their youth, though we know they are not going to get any larger helping than we did.

Or it is covetousness, which is a rather nasty brand of desire. Since desire is a normal feeling shared by the human race, I think to be covetousness, it's got to be obsessive desire. That, of course, is also a definition of lust, a sin more at home in old age by that definition than the usual limited one. It's not that sex isn't at home in old age but that sex isn't sin, and obsessive passion takes a lot of energy.

Lust is compulsion, a cancer that grows to displace healthy desires, appetites, and pleasures. Maybe its gerontological counterpart is envy.

In old age, envy can go to the head of the class. When you are collecting losses, you don't enjoy seeing others collect better things. You envy what you see, so you don't look closely.

I remember a time when I was driving a charming and brilliant young concert pianist from an engagement in one city to one in another. His name and the reason I was doing this escapes me now. What I recall is driving westward through Kansas farmland in the late afternoon, envying his gift. The sun descended to the horizon, and I exclaimed at the wonderful colors in the sky. He said, wistfully, "You're fortunate. I'm totally color-blind. It is all grey to me."

Deceit is rampant in this culture (as in any) and it doesn't get left behind when we move to retirement housing. Deceit is plain old lying, when it is at its ugliest, in slander (which the Bible calls false witness) and gossip, in spreading rumor and misleading the ignorant. It is most dangerous when practiced on oneself. We lie to ourselves when we deny the truths we know, and when we won't find the truths we need to know.

Anger also takes a good deal of energy, and in old age has a tendency to harden into hatred and resentment, fossils that must be chiseled out of oneself with many strokes, over a long time.

These are cold sins, replacing anger's destructive fire, but they are every bit as deadly.

If I may use an oxymoron, sloth is pretty active in senior circles. There isn't any sin in sleeping late, or having somebody else make your meals, of course. That's not sloth, but not bothering to think certainly is. Not bothering, not caring, forgetting to wonder and refusing to be concerned are the works (if I can call them that) of sloth. It isn't laziness (especially physical laziness) so much as it is what C. S. Lewis called fed-up-ness, not caring about anything, giving up on everybody, and throwing all your pearls into the pigpen. Categorization is one of sloth's specialties, cynicism is its native tongue. Boredom and sloth are intimately joined. Not only does boredom produce sloth, sloth produces boredom, which is not the result of repetition, a legitimate and often effective method of entertainment and of learning. Boredom is the result of unused capacity.

Pride is the big one at the head of the traditional list, but it is also, I think, one of the most loosely interpreted of the lot. When I was very young, I thought "pride" meant being stuck-up, until I misbehaved at a luncheon and my mother asked if I didn't have any pride at all. Obviously it was something she wished I had more of, so how could it be a sin?

The sin of pride is what the Greeks meant by *hubris,* and they put it at the head of their list. I know what that meant to them: it meant wanting what belonged to the gods and being dissatisfied with being human.

It's what we mean now by "perfectionism" and/or the stubbornness that won't admit shortcomings and can't let anybody else win. It has never learned to say "thank you" and it can't be dependent gracefully. It gets pretty well summed up in the classic American need to be Number One.

I don't know where on the list you'll find rigidity and miserliness and the breaking of vows and stealing things like time and attention, or where to put manipulation and the attempt to control other people, but, believe me, they belong on it.

Ambition sometimes belongs on it, too. That is what the virtue of aspiration turns into when it falls in the mud of envy, pride, covetousness, competitiveness, greed and/or obsession. Aspiration aims for excellence; ambition aims for power. Aspiration wants recognition; ambition wants adulation.

Spiritual counselors have always pointed out that virtues carried to extremes can turn into vices. (Unfortunately, vices carried to extremes remain vices.) Some sins are virtues distorted, wrenched out of their proper graceful shape.

The consequences of these sins vary, but guilt is one of them. I mean the fact of guilt, not the feeling. There are so many people going around carrying huge bags of guilt-feeling on their backs, for things they didn't do, things they only wanted to do, things they did and paid for or corrected, and it's a shame.

There are two kinds of guilt: imputed guilt, which is felt but not earned, often loaded into the bag by somebody else. Then there is earned guilt, which is just what it says, but may not be noticed by the perpetrator.

A lot of things people feel guilty about as sins, aren't. Being too harsh a judge of oneself, however, can turn into a sin if you aren't careful. It's an example of virtue carried to the extreme of sinfulness. The theological name for it is "scrupulosity." It is a great problem for perfectionists. The whole subject needs a generous salting with the virtue of generosity, to keep it from going bad, which it easily does.

Take that old phrase, "lusting in the heart." Considering an option is not an act and involves no culpability (or credit if it is a noble act being considered) until somebody *does* something about it. A passing "impure thought" (impure? it's built into the organism) isn't sinful. After all, it is considering and *rejecting* an action that is virtue. Refusing to acknowledge a possibility can be simply running away, and often more from fear of being unable to reject, than from horror at the very idea. Real "lusting in the heart" is staying with the idea, re-running it on the mental screen, even what we might call wallowing in it. By then, it is a deliberate act, even though a mental one.

What is not a sin is considering the option and promptly rejecting it. Part of the problem of this whole subject is that there is more than one sinfulness around to be lusted after. Ambition has its lustful daydreams, hatred has its lustful hankerings after revenge, and pride (or *hubris*) has its lustings after "the things that belong to the gods," power and perfection and adulation (that's worship, or as near as makes no difference.) Self-love is certainly not sinful, but I suspect self-hate can be, with its basis often in perfectionism, its belief that "this life isn't good enough for me."

Revisions

Repentance is the cure for sins. This is not a feeling. It is change, inner and outer, change of attitude and change of behavior. It includes revision, literally re-vision, a new way of seeing. It includes the glad acceptance of your own humanity.

You can't just kick a sin or a compulsion or a bad habit out of the establishment and that's that. It will, as the parable demonstrated, come back, probably bringing its pals along. The practical way to get rid of the things in yourself you don't want there is to *replace* them.

Replace lying with honesty, which has a way of letting in fresh air and sweeping out the dirt. Replace hatred and judgmentalism and resentment with compassion, which is a warmer and homelier virtue than the word "charity" has come to mean. It's a rare form of love, with no condescension in it.

Replace envy and covetousness and greed with "thank you's." Let humility (so long misunderstood) replace the perfectionism and the ambition. Invite acceptance in, and let it bring wonder and delight and mystery with it.

Open up the tight and grasping hands of greed and covetousness and the other obsessions, to receive whatever gifts are being handed out by the world today—music or flowering nature or snowy mountains or warm-hearted people. Or storm and flood, whatever is today's specialty. It takes open hands to accept, especially to accept humanity and forgiveness and healing.

The refusal to accept forgiveness is itself a result of sinfulness. Especially in old age, beware hanging onto old guilts and grudges and even self-chastisings. That hanging-on can be *hubris,* or it may be just a bad habit. Emotional and spiritual habits are the hardest, and the most important, to change. I hope there is a spiritual statute of limitations for these things.

The sins of old age are the same old sins of all the other times of life, and all the other ages of mankind for that matter, maybe a little less violent among seniors and maybe a bit harder to budge. Whatever harm sins cause, the worst is always to the sinner. Whatever miracles virtues work, the best is for, and in, the one who holds them dear. By this time we should have learned to prize them.

"all regrets should have expiration dates . . . "

THIS DAY

Let each day drop from my hands when I have used it.
Let me take up each day new when it begins,
with empty hands — empty to handle this day,
    its pain and pleasures
    its work and wonders
      its puzzles

Days that have been are part of my bones, their
strength,
    of my heart, its fire,
    of my mind, its skills.
      I need not grasp them.

Let me give yesterday back to the One who lent it,
leave tomorrow in His hand who will provide it.
Only then am I free to live this present,
    its learning and forgetting
    its loneliness and laughter
      brightness and blindness
      as they come.

"However things are, they won't stay that way."

METAMORPHOSES
(after Escher)

*Ovid was certainly right: Things keep turning
into other things — children into people
who are barely acquainted with you, parents
into legends or injunctions.*

*Babies are born reaching for difference
if the cord is firm to love or to themselves
yet if we say their change is painless
we have forgotten how it was.*

*Undependability, in oceans or slow-
shifting continents is the one dependable.
We try to retard glaciers, splint rivers' channels,
cast roses in plastic, freeze the remembered dead.*

*We bury assets under mattresses to draw
no interest. Blessings rust in paper napkins,
wind-blown in dooryards, because the gain
we think we want is change we fear.*

*In spite of us, virtues harden to vices,
at least to stones that love must stumble over.
Innocence turns weapon, caring becomes control,
faith twists into* jihad.

*Escher drew truth in sliding birds and fish
in angels turning devils and* vice versa.
Identity is vulnerable.

LIVING WITH LOSS

The Other Fact of Life

When we used to speak of the "facts of life," we usually meant the facts of birth, and what leads up to it. The other fact of life is death, and what evolves from it. In young years, birth is the thing that gets most thought about, one way or another. In old age, death takes center stage, for some similar reasons.

Old age does confront us with the facts of loss and death, but neither is restricted to old age. The young know these things, as we did. We still wear their scars, and new wounds disturb them. The effects of loss are cumulative, and old age seems to concentrate and intensify things.

The "size" of a loss can only be assessed by the person who suffers it. It is cruel to consider, for example, that the death of a child's dog is not as "important" as adult losses. When the lost object carries away the emotional investment of the loser, it is major, and to belittle it is to insult a memory and deny a need. Emotional pain *is* what it is experienced to be, and nobody ever declared a contest for pain.

Losses never occur in a vacuum. They happen in a context. If the child whose dog dies is a lonely child, a misunderstood child, if that loss takes away love's only source or opportunity, the result is utter desolation. That desolate child lives yet, in all of us, whatever our age.

If history is the story of people's accomplishments, it is equally the story of their losses and defeats, but in the general history we focus on achievements. In our own histories, we tend to concentrate on the losses and the might-have-beens. We look at other lives (contemporary or legendary) set in a vast horizon, and at a distance. We view our own indoors, looking out windows to the rest of the world. It isn't that this is a wrong thing to do, this is the only thing we *can* do. We have to keep in mind that we're doing it, and that it makes comparisons impossible.

A young man was telling about his discovery that when he envied the confidence and assurance of others, comparing them with his own fears and insecurities, he was comparing total unlikes. He said, "I was comparing their outsides with my insides. I only saw how they looked. I only knew how I felt."

This happens to seniors when they compare the present they feel with what they see of others' lives or recall of their past. Loss and disability, whatever "size," tend to hide the horizon; if these occupy old age, they may be all we can see. Pain isolates, and grief is a kind of exile.

Kinds of Loss

Loss is a change we suffer, but change is also somehow loss, and it brings a kind of grief, even when it's change we like.

We have talked about the various kinds of loss that tend to congregate in old age. What is true of bereavement applies to all loss. The difference in degree may be great, but the responses and side-effects are similar and coping with it calls for the same efforts.

Loss may not be the catastrophe (or, possibly, release) of a death. It may be mental eroding of disease in a loved person, or time's attrition of emotional and social networks. When relationships start disappearing, you become more aware of all the vanishings, deaths of movie stars whose images once walked through your days, buildings torn down, social structures gone. These disappearances remind me of my mother's birthplace, a town swept away by one of the floods of the Mississippi, acting for Heraclitus' river of change.

Less obvious but more urgent, discussed in an earlier chapter, is loss of things you looked to for your sense of significance, and of self-worth.

You may most painfully lose significant people, strong relationships. Even after healing, the scars will ache, reminders of mourning, but also of what you once had. What may hurt worse is loss of what you didn't have, a might-have-been that never quite was. These lost hopes are usually hidden. They need to be carefully mourned, not shoved aside or run away from.

Loss brings, more often uncovers, unfinished business—not unfinished paintings or symphonies or acts of trade, but emotional irresolutions, words unspoken, spoken ones not retracted.

Not all losses hurt. Some are releases, even when we may not want them. A loss can be a manumission, a gift of freedom, though that can have a dark side. Release from responsibility, however welcome, may carry anxiety or unwarranted feelings of guilt.

When a life-work has reached what we call "burnout," release is welcome, but maybe what is needed is only respite, not total severance. "Burnout" is not necessarily total. Even when the abandonment of a career is totally desirable, there still can be grief at losing what you spent a lifetime learning to do. That is perhaps illogical, but feelings have little to do with logic.

The professional who is experiencing burnout may later find a place to use the proficiency, without strain. I think of a friend who was a professional counselor, retired with relief, and now puts her skills to work in her church, ministering to shut-ins. I know gladly retired teachers who enjoy new areas of teaching. Artists seldom really retire, but often turn their art to new directions, experimenting, daring new techniques, new visions.

This doesn't apply only to professionals. Whatever you leave behind with relief may be returned to later with joy, especially if it is found in a new guise. Old age can probably be most rewarding when it enables the answering of an old calling in new ways, and in a freedom unavailable before, to risk and experiment. Life is change, at any stage, but in old age that change becomes more dramatic. It's a time of loss and of gain, but the gain has usually been gradual and unnoticed, while the losses come sharp and sudden, or our perception of them is sudden. It is a good idea always to keep the gains in sight if you can. You do have more choices in some parts of your life, less in others. The need to choose can cause a vague fear, a low-level anxiety, that Kierkegaard called "the dizziness of freedom." This anxiety is a part of adventure, lack of it can send people looking for it. Don't try to run away; you'll get used to what is.

This Death

Death is the big one. Death of a loved person is like being run over by a tank. However normal it is (to be expected in every life, sooner or later) it is still critical trauma to those who must live with the event and its aftermath.

The first effect is numbness, disbelief, similar in its way to the shock that comes first after severe physical trauma. This and the grief that follows when the shock eases are not just emotional disturbance. They are total: mental, physical, emotional, and spiritual. The mind can't work well, the body is at various kinds of risk. The side-effects of bereavement have been likened to those of a drug. They need to be watched.

The death of a spouse is loss of the present and of an assumed future. The death of a parent is the loss of one's own past. For the old, death of a child is also the loss of one's past as well as the future. No death is just a death; it is always this particular death. It is no abstraction, but one of the most concrete and far-reaching events possible.

Blame and guilt are fellow-travelers of grief. All that led up to the death is integral to the experience, which explains some of the guilt of the "if only" that so plagues survivors. Surely somebody is responsible for what has happened. Grief, like all emotional trauma, needs to find a way to "make sense," needs to find some meaning in the event.

Then there are grief's other fellow-travelers—anger, regret, and that useless question: "what if?" We are besieged, and want to lash out at this attack on us. We try to relive events in our minds, in a way to "prevent" the death. We feel guilty for being alive, when death has bested one close to us, and feel little guilts for our humanness that wasn't always omniscient to know his needs, or omnipotent to furnish them. We are a long way from being realistic, and not very far from being irrational.

I remember wondering if I was losing my sanity after Edward's death. I recalled an interview in which Helen Hayes said, (if I remember rightly) that for two years after her husband's death she was "crazy." That was a great comfort to me, for I thought, if that is how that great lady felt, it's OK for me. (I've long wanted to thank her for her courage to say it. This is my first opportunity.) If we "go crazy" in grief, we do it in good company.

No matter how strong your belief in an after-life, this death is painful separation now. It ends comradeship, affection, mutual support. It steals opportunity for connectedness, and all the little interchanges of a shared life that are so terribly big in their importance. It is *loss,* often at its most painful.

This confrontation with the inexorable fate of humanity also brings us up against the fact of our own death, and the fear it raises. No faith prevents this, though it can lessen terror. This fear (call it resistance if you'd rather) is not intellectual but physical, an inherent part of us. From conception on, the purpose of every healthy cell of my body is that my life continue. Deny it as we may, the fear of death is there, coloring our response to life. It colors the perceptions and behavior of those around us. Sometimes this explains what we don't understand.

The Work of Grieving

We fight a cultural denial of death that will not let us talk about it as we need to, think about it as we must, cry about it unexpectedly. All this isn't something to "get over." It is to be gone through, toward something, somewhere, if you don't know what. Grief is not a pathological state but the human condition in healthy response to deep loss. It is a normal and natural part of living, but our world doesn't teach us how to do it.

The time of grieving is full of symbols, large and small. Small ones may be most telling, triggering emotion unexpectedly. They have to be lived with, along with the necessary decisions that no one else can tell you how to make and the questions nobody warned you about.

When, and how, do you clean out the closet? (Don't let anybody else do it, no matter how long you have to wait. It doesn't have to be done all at once, it doesn't *have to* be done at all.) How do you observe the special days? What do you do about the fact that eating alone is rough? How do you recover lost initiative? How long before you stop crying suddenly? Why do crowds seem to be walls instead of people?

Why do you talk to the bedroom wall and the kitchen curtains? (Because you need to talk, and they are there. Do it.) Should you stay home or go out? (Either, but for good reason.) Is it OK to talk to him, write letters to him? (Yes, it's more than OK.) Why do you handle big things well, then come apart over the tube of toothpaste you two hadn't used up? (Because you are human.) How can you keep from remembering the times you fought? (You can't, and for goodness' sake don't try to.) Why do you feel so vulnerable? (Because you are.)

There are basic needs for the work of grieving, few but vital. From others (somebody, but who is not important) you need attention, being heard, being allowed to talk as much as you want to, if possible a shoulder to cry on, compassion, and acceptance just as you are. Role-models and mentors are wonderful if available. From yourself you need: respect, understanding as you can manage it, freedom from distorted expectations, compassion, acceptance just as you are.

There are those who say faith will sustain us, but "faith" has almost as many working definitions as "love," so has lost meaning. I am not sure, myself, what faith is, but it isn't an anesthetic, and was never meant to be. It does not deaden pain.

When Edward died, the man who was my best friend and husband for over four decades, a friend said she didn't worry about me because she "knew my faith would see me through." She ought to have worried. I was in pain, confused, lost, and sometimes despairing, for all that on the surface I kept doing all the "right" things. If I had faith, it didn't clear my confusion.

I think in time God did these things and I, with hard work

and help from friends, did them. So I tend to define faith as keeping on when you aren't at all sure there is a reason to. I recommend doing that, but it isn't easy or comfortable and it often feels impossible.

Along with the man, I lost my own sense of significance. I knew I mattered greatly to him. I am sometimes unsure now that I matter much to anybody, but that is in my darker moments. Certainly I am not important in that way to anyone else. It is simply something I can no longer have, though the fact that I did have it helps me find my significance to myself. My present state is the human condition.

The lost person couldn't be regained, but I had to regain myself. Loss of a love is grief; loss of one's self is terror.

Grief is not a matter of thinking, not exactly a matter of feeling. It is more like listening at the edge of a black hole. There is a sense of waiting for something, and of being pulled into nothingness. It is a sign not of weakness but of survival, not something to be coped with but itself a coping mechanism.

Ours is probably the world's only culture that doesn't provide ways of dealing with grief. This means that in our ethos, the bereaved is likely to be deprived of support and understanding precisely when these are most needed. If your grief is not acknowledged, you feel cut off from the community.

Grieving is done in two worlds, a social one in which only strangers die, and your own, which death dominates until you dethrone him. You do this, eventually, not by rebellion but by recognition, by finding death to be as much a part of nature as birth and growth, as much a part of the world as you are. This is not done quickly or easily, for while it may sound intellectual it is an emotional and spiritual process.

Don't try to stifle the feelings that well up from time to time, even long after the event. Giving yourself permission to feel what you now feel means permission to go beyond that feeling when you can. The only road to a new life goes through the grief, not around it.

Although grief is not a thought, people offer us thoughts to counter it. (The logic we offer to grieving friends is really aimed at our own discomfort and frustration at being unable to relieve their pain.)

Later on, the mind may be able to rejoice at having had what it has lost. At first, all the state of shock can do is perceive the incredible, and nothing else can act in that perception. It forbids the mind's entrance. That does come in time, but not easily. It is when heart and spirit surrender their emergency roles that the mind must labor. Yes, it does have work to do.

The loss of someone you love is pain—serious pain. It needs healing, not cure. There is no cure. But note what that says: "someone you love." As hard as it is to lose being loved, it is harder, and more serious, to lose the act of loving. I miss the love of those who are no longer with me, but I miss more the opportunity to love them, with my own kind of loving, not simply being a source of love someone has pre-defined.

The work of grieving is striving toward acceptance of what is. It is not liking it, not agreeing to it, not even resignation. It is recognition of the truth, and giving up attempts at control.

An important part of grief-work is learning to define our sadness, to recognize our distractedness and disorientation for what they are. It is important to be able to differentiate grief, which is healthy, from depression, which is not.

Even the loneliness is not as simple as it seems. It can be three simultaneous processes. There is the being alone, a fact of existence, one that has been and can be lived with. There is the loneliness, which goes deeper, but is an acquaintance known from childhood. There is the missing of the one who is gone. This is the source of hurt which can't be alleviated by things which help aloneness, even loneliness.

I don't advocate any kind of stoicism—that is what we already attempt too much. It doesn't make room for whatever love is offered you. It may not even leave room for God. There are times in a life when you have to find a place where you can lick your wounds, and let them begin to heal. It will be a dark place, but it need not be cold, and it should always be a place you can come back out of again.

To live with a death is to endure change. To change is to die a little bit. Both lead to an unknown that may well in time be victory, even a kind of glory, and will surely be a part of growing, even if only to find what is not the right direction.

We speak of the work of grieving, which is what it is, not the self-indulgence it is often thought to be. Of course it is painful, but that pain is as inevitable as birth-pangs. It is work that must be done, and if it isn't, then it will lead to the lingering ache of the unresolved.

Grief-work left undone colors and distorts the rest of our emotional engagement with the world. Done well, it leads to easing of the hurt, and in time to healing.

Coping and Healing

In dealing with grief, we have to re-arrange priorities. In the face of what is so big, we find ourselves dropping the trivialities, and this is a healthy thing.

When a friend came to be with a woman immediately after her husband's death, the widow apologized for the disordered state of a household, after it had sheltered several grown children. The friend said, "Of course the house is in confusion. You've just had an earthquake here." That earthquake does similar things to inner order, so you need to find what in your life is solid enough still to be standing.

In the aftermath of a close death, there are two traps to avoid: compulsive busy-ness and excessive withdrawal. To stay too busy to grieve is to put off the inevitable, leaving it until it is harder, and more dangerous. To withdraw too much from the world and our proper concerns is to deny ourselves what can lead us through this time safely. What we need is balance.

Resolution

Old age brings losses and diminishments, but seldom are the losses total or the diminishment in all dimensions. You can bewail losses (you should, to a degree) and overlook treasures that may lie at your hands for the taking, if you will look in front of you instead of over your shoulder. You can know diminishment (you will, whatever you do) and fail to notice the things about yourself that are still capable of growing.

The spiritual aspect of grief-work is often overlooked, but it is urgent, and not touched by the poems on consolation cards. As grief is not just a feeling but a whole state of being, so faith is not certainty, love is more than sentiment, and hope is not expectation but a way of acting, a matter of "keeping on keeping on."

Faith and love and hope go much deeper than thoughts and feelings, their effects are more far-reaching. These gifts are usually interacting necessary means to that resolution which is the aim of grief-work.

Resolution is not mere resignation. It is multi-faceted, and more than the sum of its parts. It includes reconciliations—with facts, with people, past and present.

For the grief finally to resolve itself, there must be some kind of closure and a new determination, a new direction taken, onward from the loss, forward, yet not in denial of it, not away from it.

Resolution comes when the loss and grief become a part of your ongoing life, no longer in a compartment but an integral part of who you are. Then the grief worked through can spread through your life, to deepen and sweeten it. We can, instead, let ourselves be made bitter. We have that choice.

If we have mourned, it is because of what we had, because at least at one time we were blessed—even if only with hope. Every death is the result of a life's existence; every burial is the result of having been born; and every bereavement is brought about by a relationship. All real love stories end in tragedy. Pain is the price we pay for love, as it is the price of life.

Grieving done never totally disappears. The resolution is its becoming a part of life's fabric, and always a part of the survivor's identity.

Now I need to learn how to play my life as a solo instrument. For a time I was used to playing in an orchestra, for most of my life in a wonderfully demanding duet.

That I am a widow has become part of my everyday life. Being Christine began long before Edward came into that life and is lasting past his presence, but that he is gone never quite fits.

"grieving is done in two worlds . . ."

NOSTRUM

People who say that time heals
lie. Time only dilutes experience
by the muddy water of fact.

Hope, too, is soluble. Bitter can concentrate
like salt. Gravity takes pain down
to be buried, but pressure refines it.

If healing is done, it is not by
any abstractions. Time hones a thin edge,
sharp, on broken bone. We carve with it
or butcher. We
are the only surgeons.

"Grief is . . . like listening at the edge of a black hole."

WALL PRAYERS
(Vietnam Memorial, Washington, DC)

Gifts at the foot of a wall shining black,
reflecting a rose, papers, messages.
Whatever they say, they are prayers —
prayers, sometimes, to a god unknown
though we thought we knew Him.

These are like the tightly folded papers
forced into cracks of the wall remaining
once a temple in far Jerusalem.
Prayers for the dead are never for the dead

who no longer need them, whatever
was waiting beyond that dark wall.
They are prayers for ourselves
who need them, who need to say them.

And the things we think we have said to God,
unknown or long learned, are addressed
to a mortal partly known who is no longer
to be addressed, and who will not answer
in any language we can translate.

COMING OUT OF THE CAVE

A Chain of Changings

"Tide" is itself a metaphor for change. The whole process, not just of old age, but of living, is like the sea, a succession of tides, a chain of changings.

My favorite Greek philosopher, Heraclitus, noticed that, and claimed that everything in life flows, all is flux. He is best known for saying that "you can't stand in the same river twice."

Now we know what he didn't, that at its heart even the planet we live on is not solid rock, and that what looks like solid rock isn't really solid. There is no solid anything. Heraclitus knew what he was talking about: everything flows.

I think human beings are better equipped for handling change than for handling monotony. It is only when change happens too fast or is too drastic that we have trouble dealing with it.

It's been going on all your life. Birth was your second big change, and you probably didn't like it. Birth happens when the environment is ready, not when the subject chooses. Like old age.

The first big change was conception, essentially the change from nothing to someone. The big one ahead is death, which defines risk and colors our attitude to change. While change has been a recurring fact, it has usually been possible to ignore it, to do it half-heartedly, our minds on other things.

Though we may see change as threat, if it doesn't happen, we go looking for it. What old age gives is more experience in doing that looking, more skill in adapting and assessing, and probably less patience.

Caves in the Cliff

Riding along Cave Creek, deep in the Chiricahua Mountains near the Mexican border, I looked at the many caves in the karst limestone, opening high in the cliffs. I thought back to when those caves might have offered shelter to any people who lived there a long time before us. I tried to imagine what it would feel like to live in those caves. I felt the assurance of their walls, but then I also felt the pull they would exert to keep from you from going any farther. They were security, but they could become traps, and finally tombs.

Looking back over the world's human history, it seemed to me that people have always been coming out of some kind of caves. In some ways, this stage of life can be finding caves, or coming out of them.

Sometimes we need something like caves to retreat to, while we regain lost strength of one kind or another (I think of convalescence), but they are dangerous places to stay in too long. Always count on coming out again.

In some ways, too, this time is like adolescence stood on its head. Then, our bodies were changing; it was a little bit frightening, but mostly exciting, because the changes offered promise. Now our bodily changes are frightening because they seem to take away promises. Those early changes were toward expansion; as far as we can see, these are toward diminishment.

In some cultures, the broader view from old age has been called wisdom. There is logic in this. Since wisdom requires a certain amount of experience, seniority is at an advantage, but of course, seniors can just as well be silly and superficial. No one is immune to that at any age.

From infancy onward, human beings need the tension of security and adventure, the chance to question and to hold firm. Now adventure faces us, and our security and certainties seem to be slipping from our hands.

The outer changes that seem so inexorable are less threatening than the inner ones, but even in old age, you don't just suffer change, even when you can't avoid it. You can choose to do it. You can usually choose how you do it.

Change Is a Law of Nature.

Change is a natural law, but don't assume that change is good just because it is inevitable. On the other hand, don't assume that change ought to be resisted on principle. We always need to reserve the right to open the package.

Successfully resisting change is possible, but not often probable. What we do have, within limits, are choices as to how we feel about such things, and how we will respond to them. Respond is what we need to do, but sometimes we only react.

Reaction is immediate and unthought, like your leg's motion when your knee is hit with a rubber hammer, so the cliché "knee-jerk" has almost become part of the word "reaction." Responding is slower, thought about, decided. Reacting has little to do with choice. Responding has everything to do with it.

Changing has consequences, but so does not changing, and you can't opt out, because not choosing *is* a choice. Then choices follow choices, until they become a direction. You can resist a change, or use it. You can embrace it or keep it at arm's length. You choose what you will do with *each* change, and your choices add up, and make you who you are. Choice takes courage, which is not a matter of heroics but of steadfastness.

Maybe you are resisting change because you are trying to hang onto something that has already gone, or maybe you want a change because you are trying to grab what you wish for. In either case, you may throw away the present, with its demands and its opportunities. The present is where your choices are.

Staying-put often feels safer than changing, but remember World War II's Maginot Line, the fortification built after World War I, meant to protect France from invasion. War had changed, and the Maginot Line hadn't. *Blitzkreig* was the new form of war, and no such fortification could hold it back.

A Maginot life is one that keeps preparing for what has already happened, and therefore is vulnerable to the unimagined, the unguessed, that is to come.

Changes come in all magnitudes, forms, and urgencies. They can be temporary or permanent, but what seems permanent often turns out to be temporary, and *vice versa*. Change of form is obvious, change of substance may be less visible, more important.

Even the changes in ourselves, inner and outer, are likely to be more complex than we are aware of. We may fear change because we feel that it would take us away from being ourselves, but sometimes it is only change that can ever take us back to being who we are. Indeed, changing may be necessary if we are to become our true selves. Our lives are this process, of becoming who we are, and recognizing ourselves. I'm not talking about what people a few years ago called "finding their identity," which implies something static. We are process. In our best changes, we don't so much find ourselves, like the lost car keys, but we manage to join up with our marching selves. This has always been going on, and it doesn't stop in old age.

One of the best things about changes is that they make impossible even the attempt at perfection.

If you meet every change with whole-hearted rejection, you are going to miss the opportunities it offers. It is good to leave at least a crack in the door for that. You never know what might slip into your life, bringing what you never would have thought of. I think of my life as a writer, and I'm sure some unwelcome changes made possible what I've enjoyed most. The difficulty with the standard advice to new writers, "write what you know," is that it implies a restriction that isn't there. What you know changes.

Change Is a Law of Relationship

If you try to hang tightly onto the honeymoon, you lose the marriage (and of course the honeymoon, too). Human beings are not built to sustain any single intense emotion, or any set of them. If you try to keep the parent-child relationship as it was when the children were babies, you lose the babies anyway, but fail to gain the mature friends they might have become for you. If you try to cast a friendship in concrete, you lose the nuances, the developments, the deepening. If you could keep anything static, you would make surprises impossible. There would be no place for adventure to sneak in, no room for growth. This way lies rigidity and boredom.

Willingness to change is necessary for any kind of development. In the Gospel, we are told to "become as a little child" but this never meant you were to give up maturity, throw out any wisdom you might have gathered. No creatures are as constantly changing as little children. To be as a child is to re-enter the process of becoming. The attitude of healthy childhood is reaching, questing, risking, exploring, trying what has not yet been done, tasting what hasn't been tasted, touching what hasn't been felt. The child is open to what it doesn't know yet. Although it may approach the new with suspicion, this is not at all the same as pre-conceived rejection.

Think about real children. What is the one thing you can be sure they won't do? Stay the same. They are constantly learning, growing, running eagerly ahead to the next stage.

At times, children want repetition ("Read it again, Daddy") as a kind of ownership, which is a kind of security. When I know a story well, it becomes mine; when things are done in ways I am accustomed to, they feel as if they belong to me, but this is misleading, for people don't want that ownership instead of new things, they want it in addition to new things. This is a natural greed necessary to growth. Staying put and being satisfied are not what we do well. At any age. We want to possess, but we also want to acquire, and sometimes there is no choice but to give up what we have, and learn to make the new thing ours. In the end, a child always goes on to new things. Even if the teddy bear survives, it is an emotional fossil.

Rote resistance and rote obedience are equally ways of being controlled by others, so you need to stay flexible enough to keep from merely reacting. The essence of healthy dealing with changes is choice, and rigidity takes away the ability to choose. Outer change can be trivial, but inner change is your attention rechanneled, your purpose re-directed, and it needs to be considered carefully.

We have proved that we can adapt, we can develop, we can see from more viewpoints than one. Our survival with mind and spirit intact is verification that we are not the stick-in-the-muds that some younger people may assume we are because our bodies are not as lithe and our joints are not as flexible as theirs. There does exist something very like an arthritis of the mind, even of the spirit, but it has absolutely no relationship to the metabolism of calcium or how long the mind has been around.

Change Is Spiritual Law

I wish I knew what saint said: "The law of God is change." It looks that way: change is the one unchanging thing in all God's creation, but of course that doesn't mean all change is from God.

Sometimes we feel that God himself has changed. Then we must ask: how true was our vision? God doesn't change, but eyes that looked for him shut against the light, ears that listened turn to other voices, hearts close on what they would keep, afraid he will take it away, confusing God with death.

Our danger is rigidity, a different quality from firmness, from being steadfast. We can become mental fossils, ideas turned to rock. Even emotions can so stiffen that what we think are our feelings are only the remembering of how we used to feel.

It is even possible to become a spiritual fossil, a living spirit turned hard, cold, unalterable. In all that we are, we are meant to grow, and to grow is to change. Even our prayers ought to change, because prayer is never just a set of words we learn to say. Prayer is a directing and focusing of our attention, a way of listening, not with the ears we tune to radio but with the ears that can hear any still, small voice that speaks within us. Prayer is even a way of seeing—seeing the world and everything in it *sub specie aeternitatis,* under the aspect of eternity.

Like the relationship with anyone else we love, our relationship with God should be a changing one, widening and deepening, becoming more receptive and intense, becoming less artificial, less confined, even to religion.

For all its concern for the treasures of the spirit, the church is still to some degree a prisoner of the culture it lives in. At first, it was a disturbing ferment in the rigid, imposed "peace," of the Pax Romana, but when the church itself grew to temporal power, it was so vanquished by the spirit of the age that it *became* the culture, to its eternal cost and the anguish of men and women, within it and without.

Sometimes, since then, it has been hard to tell church from society, when their goals and values looked the same. Not all change is of spiritual worth, but then not all stability has been spiritually supportive, either.

However, all our changing, freely chosen or forced on us, spins around the one unchanging being—God. Our perception of that centrality is not restricted to church experiences. The church exists to manifest and teach the love of God (his to us and ours to him) and all the rest comes under this, but if the church could stay exactly the same, it would really be changing, because its context would inevitably alter.

Even a church can't stand in the same river twice. And neither God nor our life with him is restricted to the church.

The Art of Change

The challenge of change is the dare to make something new, to substitute an experience for the pre-existing one, to replace habitual reactions with spontaneous responses, to turn away from the familiar in order to confront or accept the unknown. We are asked by this time of life to discard the habitual, to leave off much of our reviewing, in order to create.

We grow and change constantly, but our past is always present in our future, as the beginnings of this present experience were contained in our past.

Achieved old age has been expensive. It cost much effort of our minds and hearts, much energy and attention, much of ourselves. It should be valued more than any unthinking risks of our youth, when we hadn't noticed death waiting in the wings and didn't yet know what being alive is worth. Survival is never automatic. It is the result of art, determination, good luck, good genes, and probably the grace of God, remembering that grace is gift, not merit. Our new limitations may force us to discover resources once hidden by abilities now lost. Bodies seem to have time-limits, though not closely defined, but this may not be true of our minds and spirits. We have to go forward, but to go *only* forward is to discard resources, give up the identity that we launched from. Now the present rules, sometimes a tyrant, but like all tyrants, its reign is limited. This present will change, too.

The past is ours to use as we can, itself an instrument of change. It is not a pyramid to house mummies in. Our chief responsibility is to live, and that is always a dynamic process, not a static condition. There is no arriving.

Old myths are leaving but new ones are burrowing in, like a mole in the garden. We must watch for them. Reality may not be comforting but it's safer than denial or illusion.

Keep waking up new. To perceive in new ways means to expect differently. You aren't through growing, living, maybe fighting, surely delighting. Keep willing to dare. *Carpe diem* is not addressed only to the young. Wherever we are in a life-cycle, it is life itself that keeps saying to seize the day—and to let go of the day. This is the dynamic of healthy living, it is the art of changing.

What we are trying to do now and what we used to do are different, yet not totally different. It is the same person, yet at a different place, with different knowledge. We have to be both flexible *and* stable. The flexibility requires acceptance and willingness to surrender control. Stability asks a center, an inward rootedness, and we can't root in the surface of anything. Shallow roots soon perish.

Maybe the latter stages of human life can become a reprise of our childhood. If we will let it happen, this may be a second time of launching out, reaching; it may be a time to let loose long-restrained curiosity, a time again to heed the body's senses and the mind's powers, a time to surrender once more to wonder. The forces ranged against this are fear, habit, and the pressure of the culture. But count the very angels on our side.

In this culture, even now, and certainly in the past we have lived in, women have had mostly to live from demand to demand, from requirement to requirement, as events presented themselves. The more active her life was, the more this may have been true. Now we can deny some claims, examine demands, make opportunities, choose engagements. We don't have to do the next thing that presents itself, regardless of what we want or what we had planned. But I see most older women doing what they have always done, waiting for things to arrive, doing what is expected, living that old life only slightly re-arranged.

In that same past, most men lived by goals, set schedules, by the time-table of career or job. Maybe now is the time for them to do what presents itself.

There are always those who would try to force change, or at least try forcefully to persuade you to do it. They speak in abstraction, talking of "change," not of changes, when they are really trying to persuade you to make or to accept specific alterations they want done. But not all changes are good and not all are inevitable. Arthritis, osteoporosis, cancer, and infidelity are kinds of changes.

Only in the rhetoric of would-be persuaders is there a "cutting edge of progress." Cutting edges let blood, and the word "progress" doesn't specify direction. We have to change, but we don't always have to do it as prescribed by somebody else.

Like other abstractions, "change" doesn't exist in the real world you live in. What you must deal with is occurrences of change, changings. One at a time. Some are easy, and a lot of them feel good, at least after you've done them. Sometimes the happenings of change take place so gradually we don't see them.

When you are dealing with an abstraction, you can only take it whole or refuse it, but if you are facing individual events, you can decide what you think about each. Never accept or resist change as an absolute. Change for the sake of change always

111

needs examining. People may insist you have to change, and they are probably right, but you can and must ask: *"What change?"* Chew well before swallowing.

Old age is lived on a frontier, close to the boundary of life and death, of being and oblivion, between known world and unknown wilderness. Such a boundary is what a frontier is, for all the heroic mythology about pushing civilization further, taming wilderness. All that really gets pushed ahead is that boundary, and it's only moved, not obliterated.

The chance of change has always been the spice of life, as well as its threat. We sigh and say, "This is the way it is," and that's true, but "it is" is a sentence of limited tenure. It may sound final, but there are chinks in its solidity. "The way it was," is by contrast a sea-battered cliff even birds won't light on. You don't have to roost there.

Whatever the zodiac or counselors have to say, the story of our lives is written by who and what we are, using the pen of circumstance. The persons we become are shaped both by the lives we have lived and those *we are living* now. Be careful—and daring—you're still making your life, for better or worse.

Back to our friend Heraclitus: he taught the perpetual change of all things, the only abiding thing being the logos, or orderly principle, according to which the change takes place.

It is all an eternal pattern of interacting possibility and attraction, as intricate as that of electrons in an atom, of atoms in a molecule, of stars and planets, comets, all the dark and bright dancers in the Great Dance of the universe.

"not choosing is a choice... "

DENDROLOGY

Trees write inner history
spin circles of the years
judged within their substance.
I wonder if our souls draw rings
archives of dry and leafy seasons.

Crabs cast shells outgrown
at risk to make more ample ones.
The time of change is vulnerable.
We can choose to stay cramped but
somewhere in us lack is recorded.

"It is life itself that keeps saying to seize the day, and to let go of the day . . . "

LOT'S WIFE

Pulled by ravelled threads of old robes, by keepsake strings
of beads, grudges, guilts, pain no longer mine,
I held back, picking the scab on yesterday.
It was too hard leaving when maybe what I left
was all I'd have. It is all I'll ever have.

It wasn't even that I sighed for Sodom.
Sodom wasn't that great. It was having to go on
not knowing. Not knowing was the waste I saw ahead,
ash and dust, so I stood here. I stand here still,
still in this tangle of thirst and thorns, held
by my own dragging feet, reduced to a landmark,
my memorial of tears without eyes.

The trouble was not so much that I looked back
as that I was afraid to look ahead. Future
is cloud. My stone foot couldn't stand on it.
I rooted in a wilderness I had to go through
but didn't have to choose. Refusing is
choice. When we clutch at what is not
we are doomed to drown in dust.

I stopped to cry in sight of the rubbled past
forever, or until God bathes dead earth
with unaccustomed rain and I dissolve,
a salt river flowing
across the plain toward refuge that
I would not look for.

"To live is . . . not a static condition. There is no arriving."

RETURNING

Seasons circle we travel
as Sappho wrote time passes
returning is not quite returning

We have wound round the sun and that winding
has been voyage without reversal
ours are one-way tickets

What we departed has not stayed
it has spun with the planet and spinning
has changed its shape or its content

We are always coming back
to what is there no longer
and what seems like going away

may at last take us home
to Him who never changes
the center
the one fixed point

III

LEARNING TO FLOAT

Sometimes memory tries to stand in the same time twice. It can't do that, but it can do better things. Unwrapping the gift of old age, we find puzzles: time, with its simultaneous rush and drag; memory, with its tricks and wonders. Can you go back? Should you try to? How?

TIME TRAVEL

Time and the River

A professor I know claims that the real theme of every poem ever written is *time*. I'm not sure he's right, except that it is impossible to think of human life or experience outside of time. Even a poem written about something else is written *from* the human experience of time.

We perceive by means of our common metaphors, and sometimes they mislead us. We think of time as a stream flowing past, as Heraclitus' river, but that isn't exactly the way it is, or at least the way it feels. If we could think of time as an ocean surrounding us, would we experience it differently?

We seem to be stuck with the river idea, but we're not very clear about it. Time comes from a place we can't see, (behind us, then), flows past where we stand, and we watch (face) what it carries downstream. That puts the future behind us and makes the past the direction we are looking in. But it's the future that is mystery and the past that is the known. It's almost as if we are traveling in the opposite direction. Or time is.

Maybe it isn't time that moves, but we do. Or is it that our capacity to remember puts eyes in the back of our heads? The human capacity to keep the past still present in our minds confuses our idea of time. Memory is a way of standing twice, or as often as you like, in that river. I'm not sure you can separate thinking about time from thinking about memory. Time may be only an experience of memory. Yet astronomers and geologists count time back a long way before human memories were in existence.

Anyhow, time, whatever it is, is something we are, for now, stuck in. If we are to be stuck, then it matters in which part. Just to get a handle on the dimensions of the problem, think of the fact that the word "eternal" doesn't mean time going on endlessly (which is the way we think of it) but means "outside of time." Eternity is time not being. Try to imagine that !

A problem for books like this, trying to talk helpfully about your life, is that part of what they say is really about time, whatever it is, and part is about what your memory does with it.

For example, I can say the past is what you launch from, and by means of, unless you are stuck in it. Then I say that the present is but the process of launching yourself, over and over, and the future is what you launch towards, and sometimes why you do the launching. At least this way of thinking keeps *you* the one who moves, through time.

When I woke up this morning, had yesterday moved away from me, or had I moved away from yesterday?

The astronomer gives us a better metaphor for thinking about time. He uses the most recent technologies, brought into being in the last few moments, in order to see a light that burned inconceivably long ago and may have long since stopped burning. Yet he can only see it in this present moment—the "now" that was that light's future and is turning into our past.

For us, what *is* includes, and has been fashioned by, what was. This inclusive *now* is all we have to build on, and it is precious. We can leave the ground bare, but if we try to build our present life on anything else, borrowed or imagined, it won't stand.

What time really *is* doesn't matter as much to us as the way we feel it, which is surprisingly hard to pin down. The older we get, the more confusing it becomes. Sometimes we feel it racing by, little more than a blur; sometimes it drags itself painfully and laboring, like a cripple. Or do *we* race and dawdle?

What happened fifty years ago seems like yesterday, then you can't remember what you did in the real yesterday. Maybe there wasn't any yesterday. Maybe you just skipped it. Is this already Thursday?

For human beings, time is only a way of measuring life. No

matter how it feels, it can neither creep nor fly. Or flow. It isn't a river. It didn't go anywhere.

Since time is the measure of experience, maybe you just didn't experience enough to bother measuring. If it was a routine day, maybe there seemed no point in recording it. When you think your memory isn't working, maybe the lack isn't in your memory but in the life you are trying to remember, or maybe you are too distracted to find a yardstick.

If you want to make your memory better, you need to start not with time or memory but with what is going on in them. Do something worth remembering, not dramatic but worth measuring, and you will probably remember. Meanwhile, the best advice I've gotten about the problem is: "if you can't remember something, forget it!"

If it's important to remember it, the first thing to do is to relax, turn it loose.

To do that, read a mystery or a biography (whichever you enjoy) or call somebody on the phone, the way you might once have talked over the back fence or by the water cooler. Engage in a game or a puzzle. Take a short walk, but with a question to be answered: How many buds on the rosebush today? How many birds on the telephone wire? Those are just as important as things you used to keep track of.

Keep a day-book and before you go to bed at night, jot down what you did or what happened. Mine has a title: *Carpe diem!* (Seize the day!) This isn't precisely what the classical phrase referred to, but it is exactly what I mean. It's a way to put salt on the tail of the bird called Today, before it flies off into yesterday, and another bird alights. It may be a way of telling the birds apart!

As memory tightens and loosens, so does our sense of time. It fits itself into pigeonholes called past and present and into a promise called future. (Maybe *that's* what time is: pigeonholes!) Future turns into present, then gets tossed into the jumble basket we call "recent past," the real-life equivalent of the file-drawer labeled "miscellaneous." Any container with that label may hold something interesting, along with a lot of other stuff.

We've heard all our lives that "time is money," but of course we know better. Time is not a medium of exchange. When people are paid "by the hour" it isn't their time that is being bought. It's what they do with that hour. That's what our time is worth, too—what we do with it, but not money-wise.

To be sure, you can spend it; in fact you will spend it, somehow. The question is: what you will spend it for? Pleasure? Self-regard? Leaving the world (at least the neighborhood) a bit better than you found it? Will it be worth measuring?

Resting is a good thing to spend time on. So is fantasy. When I used to "daydream," my mother thought I was wasting time. I wasn't. I was spending it.

There are three ways of knowing time.

There is linear time, of which you say "I have left all that behind me." When we say that, we lie to ourselves, and a self will always avenge itself of a lie. (We engender anxiety , trying to make the leaving-behind true.)

There is engulfing time, of which we say, "All I have been is part of who I am; all I have experienced, I am still experiencing, all I have had, I possess." (I am still the same person, and I can remember.)

The third way of confronting time is doing just that, fighting it, trying to obliterate it. There are so many better fights in which to invest your energy, even your anger. This one is rejection of life itself, and a self-deceit. (Nobody can con us as easily as we can con ourselves.)

Even if you pull off looking twenty years younger than you are, you won't *be* twenty years younger. As current jargon has it: Get real!

Time is a gift you can't refuse. There is only one part of it in which you can live, the part called Now. Living in the past wouldn't be life, only a kind of mummification, but you can let your past live in you. That's where it belongs. That is living.

The Art of Remembering

Creative encounter is your best way to deal with time problems. Not your cleverness but your creativity can dig under the time-walls that imprison people, to the part of life time can't get into, the eternal (time-less), the spiritual part. This is not the same as "religious," though the two may overlap. I think religion is how human beings fit spirit to time, as, one way or another, we have to do.

Creativity is not your hands making things, not putting kits together. It is the making you do with your imagination, in your heart and your dreams (actual or metaphorical).

Now that scientists claim the presence of an observer alters experimental results, you can take physics for your time metaphor, watching it coalesce and bend under observation.

There are many slogans about remembering. Like most slogans, they are useful only as Band-Aids for small emergencies. "One day at a time" has proved to be a good way for an alcoholic to stay sober, and often it is the only way for anybody to get through a bad period, but alone it is impractical and impoverishing. Like "now or never," it sends both past and future to oblivion.

The older you get the more days you own. You are the richer for it, if you keep those days available. Your life has not turned into a photograph album. It has more dimensions than pictures: it has depth and feeling and value, it has spirit, and you can't take snapshots of those.

To turn your back on your past and your future is to discard all you have learned and all you hope for. Ours is a "now" culture, that bids us live in the present, forgetting the past. Resist the part about forgetting. Unlike Orpheus and Lot's wife, you *must* look back, but you must wrap yourself in the tissue of today while you do it.

Ours is not a happy era, and one reason is that it tends to deny the existence of nine-tenths of reality. All your life belongs to you. Your past has made you into the person you are. What you do with the present decides what you will be.

In the course of years, most of us lose things, and a few of them are valuable. We lose companionships, relationships, people. But those losses are not quite total, if you learn how to keep the past, rich and peopled, from sliding over the horizon.

Old age is a time of misplacing, not so much because there are holes in your remembering as that you are not paying attention to your life. Maybe this is as true of intangibles as it is of the car keys and the telephone numbers.

Using the past as a standard by which to judge the present is a totally non-creative way to treat it, actually a way to mistreat it. For most of us, no matter what our past was like, it deserves better. Comparisons have their uses but they are potentially dangerous to your emotional health.

The first rule of creative remembering is that comparisons are forbidden, for the simple reason that they are impossible. Creative remembering begins with now; it requires seeing everything and everybody as what it is in and of itself. Then it looks at the past the same way.

If your pet cat dies, you can't substitute another. You can only have a different relationship with a new pet, or do without one. The wonders of modern medicine can replace a hip, even a heart, but there is no way to replace relationships.

The present is where you live. If you always see it as inferior to what used to be, you are self-doomed to misery. The habit of dissatisfaction can be as addictive as drink or drugs. There ought to be support groups for people who are hooked on it.

The art of remembering is using the past to enrich the present, not to judge it. The events, places, people, ambiences, stored away in your head are still yours. You own them. There is no reason why you shouldn't quite deliberately take them out at times and engage yourself in re-experiencing them. This isn't running away from the present, this is simply making the most of all the "present times" you have gone through in your life.

I do that, for instance, with a place just east of Yellowstone Park, so vivid a memory that I can feel the sun sending its shafts of light down through the tall trees, to sparkle on the water, reflect off the leaves, and warm my back. I can hear the quiet, more serene for the faint music of the little stream flowing cold over rocks. Neither of us wanted to leave, but of course we did.

If I am frustrated, tired and bothered, I can go back to that campground and breathe in a little of the calm and smell the air, perfumed by the trees. It is one of the many riches I have stored during my years. Why should I leave it smashed on an album page?

I overheard people talking about someone recently bereaved. Suddenly one said, "You have to forget the past!" I almost shouted back, to say "No! It's true you must live in the present and you must face the future, but you don't *replace* the past with the present. Rather, you keep *adding the present to that past.*"

It's the old either/or trap. Those who assume you must choose between past and present have it wrong. Any artist can tell you his art is past training, practice, past visions as well as present skill and conceiving, all necessary. The same is true of the art of making a life. The past is where both skill and inspiration come from—our reason for art as well as our reasons for living. It is the well from which we draw meaning, values, and sense of purpose.

Each mourner and each celebrant of life must find a way of weaving together his present and his past. The combination is who you are. If you deny the past you are rootless, if you refuse the present, your roots will grow nothing.

Be Here Now

You can't "live in the past" because the past is not a place. You can only live in the here, and do it now. But you can *visit* that past, and the places it once contained.

You can take vacation trips to anywhere you have been, or anywhere you can imagine, for that matter. You do this the same way you go about taking any kind of trip: take "time out," decide when to return to *this* and *now,* then leave the *here.* Even if you come back wistfully, you will come back refreshed, if it was a place that ever refreshed or delighted.

There may be good reason to make a few such trips to what were not the best parts of your past. It won't have changed, but you will have. You may be able to see things you missed and understand things that were puzzling. You don't need a couch: this kind of remembering isn't digging to find out the *why* of things. That can be useful, but it's a different process.

Some periods in my past have left me with misunderstandings, unanswered questions. I find it can be helpful to go carefully back—with a time-limit, no axes to grind, no comparisons to make, above all, without seeking blame or vindication for anybody. This can actually be a way of *refusing to live in the past,* of adapting to the present, accepting where you are, being totally here now. Adventurers can only depart from the place they are in. If you go to visit your old home, it is because it is no longer home. Here and now is where you live, though it is in what was your home, school, work-place that your mind can touch people you miss, then return, still a part of those relationships, *and* back in touch with present ones.

I think this deliberate way of remembering is good for those whose loved ones have died. You have two choices about memories of people you miss very much. You can remember times together, how he looked and moved, with sadness because those are gone. Or, *after the first sharp loss has eased,* you can let yourself enjoy them again. They are, after all, true.

Memory is not fantasy. It is real stuff.

I don't know, but maybe even in some divorces, once the sharp anger and tearing apart has eased, you might make a deal with yourself to go back and enjoy the good times, then come back here to make different good times. Or, if you forget why you are alone, you could go back for a reminder—a very quick trip, carefully coming all the way back.

This can be done for marriages ended by death. Marriages go through stages, becoming a series of relationships. "Happily ever after" only happens in fairy tales. Joy belongs to real life, with all its changes, even because of its changes.

This going back is not at all the same as indulging in "if only," but is reminding yourself that being human together is more than worth what it cost, and that the other deserves to be honored for the truth about him, not imaginary perfection.

Even when it is a child that has been lost, I think creative remembering might be enriching and comforting. There is a sense in which children are always being lost to us as they grow up. The two-year-old that was, still is yours to wonder at, though you can't cuddle her. Perhaps if we let ourselves re-experience this way, we will find it easier to let a present child, at twelve or twenty or forty, do his necessary growing away from us.

The lost child really was. You didn't imagine her. Give yourself permission to feel what you felt, and to feel now what you feel now. The feeling is as real as experience, it is a part of experience. You have a right to it. You also have a right to let it change, when and as it does.

Of course re-experiencing what has been lost is sad, even painful. It can also be beautiful, its joy recognized; it can be a mode of thanksgiving. In our culture, sadness is taken for weakness, even for failure, and crying is something we apologize for (have you noticed?) but these are sometimes the only appropriate behavior, and better than the blanking out of memories that is throwing them away.

A bright smile in the face of tragedy can be heroic, or at least stoic, but it can be plain dishonest (first, to oneself.) The refusal to think about sad times can be a refusal to feel at all, and that is loss of our very humanity. Sad is . . . sad, but blank is awful. Sure, other people don't want you to be unhappy. They certainly don't want you to cry, since they would think they should do something about it. That's their problem; let it be. In this culture we get *machismo* mixed up with nobility, and with good manners. Some of us would give up our humanity before our stiff upper lip. That is a terrible price to pay. So, if you want to make that short backwards journey, do it. If you are old, you have probably shed too few tears rather than too many.

Life's depths and meanings are often tied up with its tragedies, and there, surprisingly, may also be found its deeper joys. The pursuit of happiness can cost too much for what it finds. If remembering is sad, that's a sign of its value.

Always-happy can be always-trivial. Pollyanna is not one of the world's great heroines. It is the tragedies that are great literature, and the ancients knew some reasons why this was so. They were human reasons, and they are still valid. Why are we, in our time, afraid of sadness but want to cry over movies and songs and stories?

We pursue happiness, we seldom pursue joy, but we can trip over it anywhere, sometimes in the darkest places, those behind us. Joy usually attends in disguise. It is often, like Christ at Emmaus, only recognized by hindsight.

Be here now, but do it with your whole self, which always includes your memories.

Climbing Backward

Sometimes what I write to "old age" seems to be saying, "don't look back," and sometimes, "go back and look at your life, know yourself, to find your best tools for dealing with the future."

The contradiction is more apparent than real. It depends on the baggage you take with you. If your luggage is tagged "if only," then you are going to try to remake history, a task best left to historical fiction. If you carry light baggage, curiosity and a desire to enrich the here and now, then what might have been a journey through quicksands becomes a voyage of discovery.

It's never "going home." Home is always now. However you try going back, don't even *think* of hiring a moving-van.

Travel into the past the way you climb a mountain: light pack, no hurry, stopping to enjoy the landscape, cheerfully enduring the rocks, You don't climb just to see what is at the top, but to see how the plain you live on looks from there. You stop to see the relationships of things in a new way, to see better the relationship you have had with yourself.

There is safeguard in the fact that you know you can't change the things you see from there. The distance is reality. Your here and now is the most necessary piece of luggage to take with you. That objectivity lets you marvel at beauty, rage at hurt and injustice, know and own your anger and your love, wonder at mystery, and find answers to some questions (never all) that were left unresolved. This way of going back doesn't let you finish what you left unfinished there, but it lets you tie up loose ends that still dangle inside.

From the mountaintop, you see things in perspective, a luxury denied us when we're in the middle of them. The (literally) re-viewed events remain immutable, but the way you see them changes, because you are not immutable.

The air up there is too thin to live in. The climb is hard. Faint hearts and high blood pressures may not survive it. I don't mean hearts that leave dire EKG tracings or blood pressures on a dial. I mean hearts that say, "don't dare," and inner pressures of the "shoulds" and the "if-onlys," of the need to control.

I take my journal along, because writing down what I feel, what I find, what I face, is a way to keep myself from falling off the mountain, and having this record lets me go farther each time. I think and feel my way back into an event or a time, and the writing makes me really look at it, while my NOW is in objective things: real page, real pen, real words. I let myself feel what I felt before, and what I feel now. They are seldom the same.

Take this kind of mountain-climbing for pleasure, but not too lightly. It can be painful, delightful, or both; it is always demanding. But don't take it too deadly seriously, either. Often it is just plain fun.

It can even, rarely, be dangerous, but what in life can't? Our most superficial actions may turn out to be dangerous. It is undertaking nothing, nothing serious, nothing difficult, nothing intangible, nothing ultimately important, that is the most dangerous thing you can ever do.

MEMORY

The elephants are forgetting everything,
but sounds sharpen in dull ears.
Eyes see through veils of present place
shadows forbidding recognition
until our sight pierces to light beyond
and color painted forever,
fragrance of long-vanished flowers
caught in the air of this room.

Memory is heavily dependent on our senses. Think how a perfume can suddenly "take you back" and a song can bring you words you thought you forgot. This fact is a tool to use in trying to remember, whether the attempt is to find a lost screwdriver or a lost idea, or to undertake time-travel *via* memory.

"time is a gift you can't refuse . . ."

SEARCHING

I lost my place, near the book's beginning,
have thumbed a thousand leaves, hunting through language,
which preserves treasures and confuses seekers.

It isn't the Holy Grail or fame I'm looking for.
I have no goal, sacred or profane,
that I know of.

I search for a direction — one that pulls me by the hand,
one whose leaves whisper what sounds like "home"
in some language.

How can I even say "find" unless there is recognition?
Is it all a long way round leading back to myself?
Is that not "home"?

"*The art of remembering is using the past to enrich the present . . .*"

THE LONG JOURNEY HOME

The scenery I pass sometimes begins to look
like the long journey home, going back
into myself, not in retreat this time
but bringing the world with me part-way
to where I live.

Only a few would want to come
with me to this place that glows
like the hills at sundown, warm stone
in the desert's winter sun.

If logic were a part of loss, if grief
could be defined, measured, compared
then advice might be embraced
but it lies like a foundling at my door,
adopted only to disrupt the life within.

The journey outward and in again
is not called progress
but I find that where I come
is a new place.

USING THE EQUIPMENT

Your Complex Nature

Tigresses and lionesses teach cubs how to be lions and tigers; in some primates, a whole community teaches the young how to become what they are to be. No one teaches us how to be human.

No one teaches us how to grow old, or at least how to do it well. There are few models to observe and little wisdom spoken, because the ideal held by this culture is not to grow old at all. Yet it is what most people are going to do. The only alternative is one we don't want.

The more research learns about the mind, the more complex a piece of human equipment it turns out to be. Memory is not the same as imagination, not the same as dreaming, yet a lot of the material you use in those processes comes from what you remember, sometimes from what you have forgotten that you remember, occasionally from your memory turned inside out.

Remembering is hard to understand. You forget the name of a friend when you go to introduce her, but suddenly, for no discernible reason, remember the name of a boy who sat in a seat three rows in front of you in the third grade. You didn't even like him. You try to think of a Spanish word, and come up with the French equivalent. You forget where you put your checkbook and wake up in the night remembering it. The more tense you get, trying to remember something, the less likely you are to recall it, but when you think about something else, it will come to you.

People worry about forgetting things when they get old, forgetting that they have always been forgetting. The difference is that they have recorded so much data in the course of years that there is more there to forget—and to remember. The remembering is more important than the forgetting.

The very word may tell us why we think it important. To remember is to *re-member,* as if things we had forgotten were parts of ourselves, and we must re-attach them to be whole.

Most of the daily forgetfulness that annoys and sometimes frightens us comes from the fact that we have other things on our minds. It's distraction during input that is likely to make us forget, more than being distracted when we are trying to recall.

Don't let anyone rob you of those riches you store in that mysterious organ called your brain, which may or may not equal your mind. Take charge of your remembering, putting all your senses into its service, tasting again wild strawberries in the woods, running fingers along the carved wood of a bed, smelling the perfume your mother used. Your memory becomes a sixth sense, as mysterious, pleasurable, and protecting, as the rest.

Connecting your memory to your senses is a way of recalling details that slip away so easily. Learn to "take a mental photograph" of yourself putting things away; tell yourself (aloud, hearing it), "I'm putting this gizmo in the bedroom closet." It won't feel as foolish as forgetting does.

We don't respect our memories and we don't depend on them; we write everything down. People had better memories before pencils were invented, when they had to rely on them. Memory is not only a tool, it is an asset and a talent. As tool, you can use it to create beauty and pleasure, as well as plans and intentions, and you can engage in the exciting mental exercise of learning. Creative remembering is a way of relishing the world you live in, the world that, living in, you can take into yourself.

By the time people take on the job of being old, some who think they know how to do it have only learned to fabricate answers, act out rituals, and deceive themselves. Their answers are flawed if they didn't ask the big questions which have no answers, if they don't know about old answers that proved wrong, much less a few which were workable. Their rituals may long ago have lost their meanings. Traditions that might have been learned from (if only to find out which were not useful) have been lost, or they have been used only as oil to calm the pools of complacency that had been ruffled by winds of change.

Learning

By old age (whenever that may be) a few have begun to ask questions of life (and of themselves) that can't be answered by ritual or tradition, or by ditching them. These people have lived in a wide-ranging and somewhat unfocused search, knowing many things are undiscoverable, but that sometimes you find the treasure when you are earnestly searching but you don't know exactly what for. They don't depend on serendipity, but they allow for it. They sense mystery, in the world around them, in whatever is beyond it, and in themselves.

For some time now, this 20th-century western culture has mostly left questions to science and learning to institutions, but science finds more questions instead of answers and institutions bog down in other matters.

The cap and gown is not a shroud to bury learning in; it is outfitting for expeditions into unknown territory. Since men walked on the moon it has been said there is "nothing left to explore," as if humans and their planet home held no more secrets. This isn't true of humankind, or of any man or woman. It is certainly not true of this world.

Somehow we've gotten the idea that learning is only a chore for children. This is a recent mistake; it wasn't around during the Renaissance. The fact is that youth is not the only time for learning, and may not be the best time for much of it. Maturity is a prerequisite for some valuable courses, formal or informal.

Learning in mature years has wonders to offer that youngsters can't comprehend, not because they lack brains but they lack the experience and observation. Learning in old age has advantages, it can accomplish some unexpected effects. People who study the mysteries of the mind find that the very process of asking questions makes it easier to deal with the unanswerable. The human mind, like a good knife, is sharpened by use on the right materials.

Contrary to popular opinion, education is not boring. It is an antidote to boredom, whether that learning is mere exposure to fact or the acquiring of skills. They are all worthwhile, if only because boredom is hazardous to one's health*, and learning can be a cure for it.

Boredom is more serious than we think. I have seen boredom produce fear and anxiety, because boredom implies meaninglessness, the non-existence of anything that matters. Meaninglessness is the ultimate threat, one that death waves like a dark banner.

Beyond this, the learning process brings real food to the hungers of inquiring and curious minds, themselves one of the great mysteries of the universe. Education shouldn't be too narrowly defined, for however it is accomplished, it can be a way to self-knowledge, self-awareness, or exploration of the world of others' ideas. What the wise have always meant by "education" is not the acquiring of data, not even "mere" thinking, but work toward wholeness, in body, mind, emotions, spirit.

We've been led astray not only by the concept of education as information-storage but also by its tacit definition as training for careers. If education is narrowed to vocational training, however advanced, this can leave the "educated" unskilled in thinking and judging, even in knowing, in the widest sense.

What is vocation without values? Can you teach values? I suspect you have first to teach mental and spiritual skills by which valuing is done, teach knowledge that is deep and ambiguous.

Ambiguous knowledge? Yes, indeed. There is danger in becoming acquainted with only one man's, or one school's philosophy or with one discipline's view of the world and its contents. It is in watching conflicts of ideas that we form our

---

*"Boredom," says philosopher Jacob Needleman "is the central disease of modern man." He goes on: "the psychological integrity of the human being is so constructed that the constant assimilation of knowledge is necessary even for its biological life to proceed properly. The physical body of man itself requires what could be called the food, or energy, or even the *matter* of knowledge." (*The Way of the Physician*, Harper & Row, 1985)

own, by keeping what seems to ring true, but remaining flexible enough, uncertain enough, yet to change.

Beyond storing facts, I think even organizing facts doesn't engage human minds enough to make them stretch and strengthen. Minds, old or young, need ideas and awareness, of their environment and of themselves. For a long time, this society tried to intellectualize the relationships, processes, and problems of human existence. Recently, perhaps in reaction, there has been a swing toward the acknowledgment and acceptance of feelings, the primacy of emotions, even ones we are unaware of.

But it is the insistence on a need for choosing between feeling and thought, between sensing and reason, that threatens the humane. So long as we think or feel in terms of one at the expense of the other, people will stumble around trying to be human in one mode or the other, when a major hallmark of humanity is their constant and inexorable interaction.

In some modes of psychological therapy, if the client finds roots of his emotional problems in his childhood, he may intellectualize both past events and present feelings, and be bewildered because he can't understand why he still suffers as much as before he acquired insight. Other modes offer the client a logic by which he *ought* to think, when he has known the unreason of his emotional state all the time.

These problems aren't restricted to the emotionally disturbed. They are not other than the rest of humankind, but represent the human condition focused and intensified.

The emotionally disturbed sometimes try to produce the "right" feelings, when the injection of some philosophic thinking might give them tools for the job. The mind, as Dr. Needleman has suggested, is an organ of emotions *and* concepts, and to be healthy works constantly with both. He says, "Meaning in life comes about only through the awakening of one's own real mind, including as a major component one's own real feelings."

Education, whether dealing with facts or concepts, whether teaching skills or philosophies, applies itself to the need and search for meaning, which in human beings never ceases and never is totally satisfied. This is the eternal quest. It is the quest itself that energizes, not having found.

Indeed, a persuasion of having reached the end of searching, of having all the answers, is the death of great religions and philosophies, and the paralysis of individual minds. The conviction of having The Answer can be stagnation that sours the waters of the human spirit by replacing healthy awe and aspiration with complacency, transforming the energy of search into self-righteousness, with its emotional and physical violence, the frightful energy of inquisition, crusade, *jihad*.

It was not very long ago that universal education was claimed as the answer to civilization's ills. If it could be had, universal education would still require that the questioning essential to learning be applied to its own processes. *What* education? Who decides what is to be learned?

Education for the mature is in essence little different from that needed by the young. It must offer more than facts and skills, as useful as these are. Good education offers to all who seek it quest, exploration, challenge to mental, emotional, and spiritual *work*. Strangely for such a work-oriented society, we tend to derogate the mind's labor, though the world has suffered more from the effects of mental laziness than ever from physical sloth. As for spiritual work, we discount its very possibility.

Real learning must handle ideas and search for reality deeper than can be seen, it must speak for wisdom and knowledge, mystery and phenomena, and always be impelled to go further, to remain unsatisfied with what is found because so much remains unreached.

In this "scientific" age, laymen want all questions at least to appear answerable. The "mysteries" we use for entertainment are not mystery but puzzles, and must have answers. Mystery concerns things bigger than we are. Real working scientists accept the fact of mystery; it is lay people, using not science but applied technology, who may claim there is no mystery. Scientists know better, for science is the search.

The Humanities

What we of the 20th century West lack most is philosophy, not for its systems of thought but for its approaches to a reality larger than ourselves. (Do we impose systems in order to hide from what seems chaotic, or do we find real systems in a real chaos?) The systems are an attempt to put time-handles on timeless things. We need them, but we often confuse the handles with what they would help us wield.

We urgently need to review the record of human thinking and wonder, the understanding and sensing of our own wanderings, the looking back on, and forward to, the wanderings of other thinkers and observers. We can whet our minds on the thinking of great ones who came before us; we can temper our fretfulness and our rages on their patience and commitment.

Education must be a road not only toward meaning, but toward a deeper knowledge of the human and the world. On that road, aging men and women may keep aware of who and what they are, in spite of what the culture, the mirror, or the demographic data might tell them.

We already noted how new retirement complexes provide entertainment, but little provision for the work of learning. There are craft shops, game rooms, hobby equipment, but where are tools for developing skills of the mind and for learning new ones? Where are well-managed libraries, not just collections of books donated by people who no longer have room for them?

Where are classrooms, text books, where are teachers of, say, the humanities? This field of knowledge and inquiry may not be useful in making a living (though this is moot), but it is utterly essential for making a life. That requires knowing how to think, familiarity with the human and the humane, valuing the heritage of one's civilization and the thinking of other ages.

A mind is a terrible thing to waste, and there are more ways of wasting one than by dropping out of high school. A mind needs use, beyond finding out *how much* and *how to*. It needs to busy itself with *where?* and *how?*, to dig into history, which is not only *when?* and *what happened?* but *who?* and *what was it like?*. History is anthropology and archeology, that address *how far back?* and *how did we get this way?* Geology is the history of our home planet, it and physics are *how does the earth work?* These look to the long story of continents and mountains, and into the nature of the elements. The first are what we must live on, the latter are things we are ourselves made of. Physics inquires into the nature of all that exists, from the sub-sub-microscopic to the vast.

The old seldom know much about biology, though they live in bodies and by means of them. How do other species do it? We need education in how to be old, not only in theory but in practice, physically as well as emotionally and spiritually.

These considerations lead us through the factual, into search among rich treasures of the human mind and heart, found in art and literature. It is these that speak of the meanings of life, and the depths of ourselves.

Not many are well taught in childhood how to be human. Now is the time to learn this, the most important subject in life's curriculum, the subject for which science can't give answers but the humanities can offer questions. In fact, old age may be one's graduate school, where we learn what life's experiences prepared us for, a learning not to be assured by degrees or fame. Education is not to be worn but used, enjoyed, as the fruit of a life's growing. We study great works about humankind, works of marble or music, of language or line and color, and we learn who we are, inheritors of the genius that has come before us and which, if we are in touch with it, we can add to in our time.

The capacity to learn and to teach are among the greatest gifts to the race. Learning as noun is treasure to be sought and valued. Learning as verb is a process that restores and invigorates, that keeps minds, hearts, and spirits healthy.

Education is not over with the senior prom or the degree on the wall; those are a beginning. Can old men and women again (still) be students? Can education help keep them truly alive? The answer to both questions is a resounding "Yes!"

Not only retirement complexes but all institutions serving the old, including churches, need to think in terms of what they are really offering, and might offer.

Though not all our learning stays current, the almost forgotten and the outdated still influence experience. Many things I have known are lost, language skills among them, yet the loss is not total. There is a place in me where they persist, like benevolent and challenging ghosts. However deep they are hidden, however shy they have become, old learnings still speak, offer gifts, resources, enrichments I am not wholly aware of.

Artists in Residence

The joy of creating, its excitement is a way of "working out" for flabby minds. Researchers exploring the human brain tell us mental work furnishes the kind of "short-term stress" that is good for us, a needed release from long-term stress that can damage nerve-cells. Wise observers have long known the remarkable effects of creative work for the human spirit. This may be more vital to healthy old-age than anything else.

Old makers can expand their works, perhaps leaving ways that have become too familiar, finding new ones. This can be a time to experiment, to explore, to find new teachers and remember those who taught long ago, or those who had, before, taught them, thinkers and makers and givers to our race.

I am aware of dresser drawers full of manuscripts, a closet full of framed canvasses, in bedrooms unused pianos and an organ. What is important is not what has happened to their users but what has happened in them. These objects are relics of more than career or pastime. They hold the riches of relationships, to community, family, friendships, loves, to students, audiences, readers, mentors, to the world. They are shells once occupied by aspiration, which is a brother to hope, once occupied by a special kind of love.

These undertakings of a lifetime, still being done or now neglected, are the stirrings and the stirrers of the minds and hearts of their creators, signals of the ways in which they know themselves. These are fields to be reaped, making this a harvest time, or they may be losses regretted. They speak of, and renew, connections to nature and to God, however either is understood.

In fantasy I sometimes see these works searching for their creators. What paintings, what manuscripts, run hard to catch up with people who have left them behind? Picture the nudes running down stairways, musical notes drifting in and out of windows, sheets of manuscript fluttering along hallways on each little breeze! Do pianos left behind mourn the hands that played them?

Some people leave a life's work to go to a different field of labor, like the golf course or the bridge table (Americans must work at their play) but some still play—musical instruments, typewriters, pencils, pastels. Play is the right word for those. An unremarked value of the arts is what they do within the artists. These can be models for others who are looking for oases in a desert they find old age to be. The dedication required by the calling to an art does more than fill free time, it fills empty spirits with purpose.

When seniors need to relieve pain, of whatever kind, they may use cultural models which are ways to become less aware, ways to "turn off." They may have been doing this long before they reached retirement, and find in these ways to combat senior stresses. Reliance on alcohol and street drugs, any of the culturally reinforced ways to handle stress, grows by the boredom retirement can be, if what you retired from was your whole way of life as well as the way you made a living.

I know that whatever you do to take the edge off of pain will lessen other feelings, will anesthetize pleasure. When pain is too sharp, you and your doctor may have to agree to settle for that, but it can lead you to mistake dullness for contentment. There is value in insisting on sharpness of experience. Without perception almost too hot to hold, so sharp we bleed a little, art is impossible, life is numbed, and humanity grows dingy.

Commitment

We need to make carefully whatever choices are left us, considering all possible options. We might take a leaf out of the book of business and industry, a leaf called "brainstorming." This is a simple process, older than business and industry, in which you first list all options, possible and impossible, withholding judgment, reason, and even sanity. This is a way of being truly creative, saving judgment, the critic's role, until later. Even then, assessing reasonableness should be done with a lot of "Why not?" thrown in.

Seniors can deny claims, examine demands, make opportunities, choose engagements. Mostly, I see them doing whatever presents itself next, which is the old life only slightly rearranged.

Real choices, carefully made, can justify a commitment that careless assumptions don't merit. Commitment is by definition an intense decision, a dedication. Commitments made at this stage of life are always "as of now," but they can justify the same kind of immersion as a life-work, and give similar rewards.

Commitment is a good weapon against the inroads of time. Affection, loyalty, ethics, integrity (what the Bible calls "righteousness" and our ancestors called "honor") can be handles for holding onto what is important.

You may inherit commitments or find them new and take possession of them, often by some kind of ritual. Never underestimate the power of a symbolic gesture. It is human nature to think in symbols.

While commitment is a total concern, it isn't an all-or-nothing way of seeing things. Like "either/or," that's a form of mental and moral laziness. It may make for stability, but it perpetuates injustices and prejudice. You're never too old to fight those things, especially in yourself.

Can you make any difference in cultural biases, derogatory connotations of language, ossified angles of perception? It doesn't look as if any one person could change those things, yet in recorded history it has happened many times. At least the one choice we always have is to try, according to our own abilities and opportunities, and the counsel of wisdom. Whether or not our actions can make a difference, we can always act as if they could.

This is a time to realize potential still dormant in us. Look for it in unnoticed possibilities, in forgotten choices, in old hopes and dreams. This is a time to make the most of the mystery we call life. Rest will be part of it. Healthy life, wherever you find it, is ebb and flow, tension and release, not the constant activity our culture calls vitality.

The beat of the heart is the rhythm of life: contract; expand; contract; expand. You can't improve on it, though you may have been trying for years. Now find the rhythm again, live by it, acting and resting, acting and resting. That is what bountiful living does. Action was never meant to be unceasing, energy never was inexhaustible.

"they sense mystery, in the world . . . in themselves . . . "

LEARNING

Let me learn from the roses in my room, let me bloom
my days, as I watch these give themselves
on their own terms.

Let me learn from ardent cactus in the desert,
glowing spines protecting it from sun, metering
its necessary light.

Let me learn from night, erasing cactus and roses,
changing the world into mystery no lamp
shines into.

Let me learn from dawn, spilling warm over the mountain
giving the world back, persuading roses
to bloom again.

Let me learn from patterns of day and dark, of weather,
how music repeats in this body that echoes
turns of the planet.

Let me learn my kinship to leaves and to thorns,
to planet and ocean, darkness of space,
brightness of suns.

I don't look for answers.
Let me remember to question.

"Old learnings still speak . . . still offer gifts . . . "

EDUCATION

The languages are lost. They have silenced,
but the landscapes they called from
can still be breathed. Facts tend to fall
through sieves, but their truths persist.

Some lessons were only prerequisites,
some tests were only to learn
if we could learn.

Most of the crafts have rusted
but making has never stopped.
The prie dieu *got lost in a moving van*
but the knees still bend.

When disciplines slack, memory plays.
Practice, as with a fiddle, may make
music from learning past.

You need reaching hands to receive with
but the hands are gift.
Most learned, perhaps, of all their skills
was lightly to stroke a face.

"a time to realize potential . . . look for it in old dreams . . . "

EXPLORERS

"Old men ought to be explorers"
T. S. Eliot, *East Coker, Four Quartets*

This is the time when we are finally free
to explore what we intended when young and cumbered,
but we launch ourselves from a different shore.
The place where we dreamed is gone —
like my mother's birthplace, gulped by the Mississippi.

Not dark continents or blue space pull us
but a land whose color we guess, one
we set out for on every journey and never reached.
We look at mountains and think of abandoned mines
but it was a different treasure we were after.

We look at ocean, and anchors we never weighed.
We can board now. Brave ships are still commissioned.
In an age of wings, their tall sails
give the word "gallant" a presence
no supersonic transport knows.

The world has shrunk around us like winding cloths.
It gorges us with facts and changes, it seduces
our ears, vision, hides the place we were going,
but we can sail to it, the destination
we were homesick for and never knew it.

GIFTS AND RESOURCES

Unwrapping the Package

Old age has come to be like the orphaned child of the black-sheep cousin in Victorian stories. No one is quite sure what to do with it, and sometimes this applies to the orphan itself. Most would be kind, but no one wants to take it in, at least not until it is demythologized and better mannered, which can mean "not obtrusive." It sometimes seems that the old, like Victorian children, are to be seen but not heard, preferably not often seen. Their presence, like the ghost of Banquo at Macbeth's table, can make others uneasy, and for similar reasons.

The Bible seems to consider long life a gift from God and a reward for living well; it doesn't tell you what to do with it. When the Bible was written, old age was rare enough, despite Methuselah, that those who got there had usually gained some wisdom in the process.

Old age doesn't come with a user's manual. You are not given maintenance instructions. While your past life may not seem to have taught skills for it, in fact many former abilities are still useful. Being able to re-train, to adapt knowledge and ability to new needs, was one of the best skills you ever developed, and is basic to this.

Of course, if you are afraid to unwrap this gift, if you put it away, while you try to hang onto a life fast turning obsolete, you will discover the stiff neck and headache of anxiety. Those aren't caused by old age but by the way you handle it.

Few of the fearful circumstances we associate with seniority are caused by it. What we think of as the ravages of age are more likely to be the result of mileage, upkeep (or lack of it), and circumstances. That is always the human condition. It is no more true of old age than of youth; it is more visible. A birth date doesn't explain most aches, pains, and malfunctions any more than it assures wisdom, virtue, or social status.

Gifts of Time

Old age is a gift of added time, added life, opportunity. It is also the gift of keeping longer all the ages you've been. You've acquired a lot of life-space for good things to happen in; you've also had some bad ones, of course, and there may be more. Meanwhile, this is a space in which to "regroup," and to heal, if you need to.

You've lost and gained, and are still doing both, but every lamented loss meant you had possessed value. There may be more gifts ahead if you aren't holding what you had so tightly that there's no room for anything new. There can even be room for experiments in spite of the fact that a good deal of your energy gets burned up by all those candles on your birthday cake.

You have added time in another sense, in the gift of leisure, a gift apparently not always desired.

Leisure's first name is Janus. Like that Roman god of the new year, it faces two ways. It can be opportunity or burden. It offers freedom to concentrate on wonders or on what's wrong. There is freedom to do what you want, but if you don't know what you want, then you only have freedom to do what you can. Even when opportunities are visible, they may be unreachable. One of the results of that endemic American illness, depression, is that the human self-start button functions poorly, if at all.

Professional writers give us a tip for overcoming inertia, when they suggest that you never leave an ongoing work tidily finished off at the end of a sentence, paragraph or, worse yet, chapter. A dangling end is provocative; a strong human urge is to tuck it in neatly. By the time that's done, the work is rolling— perhaps haltingly, but rolling.

The best thing about leisure may be its possibility of immersing yourself in pleasure and stimulation of the kind experienced by the artist or the knowledgeable connoisseur. But leisure can also stun us by a multiplicity of options that make us have to choose. It is easier to take hold of one opportunity than to choose among many.

This is one reason people talk about "killing time" when they are not pressed by it. You can no more kill time than you can kill a tape measure, but time ill-used can kill a lot of life.

There are other gifts, literally priceless ones, we take too much for granted. I think of the accessibility of things to enjoy, music, drama, literature, any of the arts. I think of beauties of nature and man-made ones. I think of affections, shared pleasure and tasks, any liking, respect, or love you don't have to keep working for.

Resources—Human

It is always a good idea to identify your resources early in an undertaking. Old age, particularly when it becomes official, is definitely an undertaking. It doesn't just happen to you, it is something you do, or it should be.

You probably have more resources than you are aware of, until you go looking for them. They are found in people, the community, and yourself. They are inner and outer, in body, mind, feelings, spirit. You can find them in your past, your skills and concerns, in found fellowship and that you build, in solitude. Vocation, being the ultimate of purpose, is a potent resource.

One early spring day in Wisconsin, a taxi driver told me how he almost dreaded good weather, because it hurt him to see the deterioration of people who had spent the winter alone. Icy walks don't make for sociability, when your bones are brittle.

People need communication, verbal and otherwise. There is no relationship without it. Maybe we need to find new ways to fill needs the vanished ones left. We have thrown out some ways of communication that did work, and still might, if we could retrieve them.

We've lost people with whom we once communicated. We can't replace them, and we can't "make up for" their loss, but we can find new relationships to give us the sense of community, even the communion, we need now. It will take openness, it will

150

take patience to let relationships develop. (Patience is supposed to be a virtue of old age, but I haven't seen—or felt—much evidence of that.) The important thing is to approach each possibility of friendship or companionship as itself, not as a replacement.

There are good things about this culture, but it teaches some bad habits. It trains us to compare everything. Comparison-shopping saves money in the food store, but comparison-shopping relationships cancels their best possibilities. Comparison-shopping personalities makes us blind to persons. When we compare one person with another, we can't see either of them clearly while taking measurements. How do you measure values, touch, companionship, beauty, pleasure? You can't see warm, living, growing, changing, unique persons, through a blueprint.

Sometimes you can learn a lot more from listening to a person than from looking. I can tell you of dancers who have trouble walking but who still dance in their souls, of mental athletes whose legs never did win contests but whose minds still leap over bars, and do it with grace and wit.

Learn really to *see* each human being you deal with, looking at what *this one person* is like, not how much he/she is like or unlike another. Allow time for getting to know this person, too, because first impressions are inadequate.

In finding your human resources, there may be some false starts. If you want someone to understand what you are going through, look toward your peers. I don't mean your age-peers, but those with whom you can share a point-of-view, allusions, ways of thinking and feeling. Those near your age won't all be close to your interests, your experience, your knowledge. The people who are resources for understanding your circumstances are the same ones, of various ages and personalities, who would understand and identify with you under any circumstances.

Don't look for one person to be compatible in all areas of living. We need relationships of different kinds, different depths, you might even say of different flavors. Some that don't go deep can be sources of delight. Some are important to share momentous occasions with. We need models, too, and mentors; we need *to be* models and mentors. Your human resources are not just for solving problems or dumping woes on. Human relationships are more complex and more rewarding than we take them to be.

Resources—Community

There are many and varied resources to be found in the community. That's the wider community, as well as the one enclosed by walls you live in. Find out what is offered by each one. If access to them is difficult, ask for help. It is an inherent part of humanity to need help at times, and it's seldom that people dislike being asked for advice.

There is a natural pattern in human life, in which we go from having to have help, through giving help, back to having to have it. It goes something like this:

—being done for—>

      —doing—>

            —doing with—>

                  <—doing for—>

             <—doing with—

      <—doing—

<—being done for—

There are now official and unofficial organizations whose purpose is to address the needs of seniors, and organizations devoted to other purposes undertake programs of assistance. These all vary in purpose and effectiveness, but somewhere you can probably find help for your particular needs.

In the civil community, look for social service agencies, local branches of national bodies, volunteer programs, churches and synagogues. Look to commercial undertakings, hospitals, retirement complexes, businesses related to transportation and communication.

When losses hurt badly, you may need help to handle them, but one of the good things about this time and place is that such help is to be had, if you are not still living in that past where needing help was thought an admission of weakness rather than admission of humanity.

There are many support groups for those with problems or in crisis. They offer mutual support and a defined program of self-training, and nurture for your helping yourself in dealing with whatever you have to deal with.

You can even form a group of your own, with its own support system and program, to deal with problems of old age. [See the Appendix at the end of this book for suggestions.]

Resource—Yourself

You may be your own best resource.

We can fall into thinking of our aging bodies as enemies who prevent us from enjoying life. But my body is always my ally and my friend, one who won't always do what I want but is dedicated to furnishing what I need. It has done this a long time. It deserves my thanks and my best care.

Many of what get called the "ravages" of old age (not all) are in fact the ravages of body-abuse, mind-neglect, emotional and/or spiritual deprivation. The effects are cumulative, and you are going to accumulate enough of some of them in seventy or eighty years to be noticeable.

Some parts of us apparently are programmed to function a limited number of times. This fact of life has to be accepted, but if it is a problem there are often solutions. Physically, I am still growing, however. My body is busily replacing most of its cells, even if some parts do wear out.

I can accept physical limitations age brings if I know that's where they're coming from, even if I don't like them, but I want to be sure they aren't from something else, and treatable.

Unlike the physical growth of muscles and girth, old age is still a growing of mind and heart and whatever human organs may store wisdom and compassion. Inner resources are even more important. They are the things you have learned, from mentors and by experiment, mental and emotional skills and the flexibility of your spirit.

In the every-day world, you need to be flexible in order to live with a minimum of trauma. You learn to "roll with the punches" and, just as important, to be open to opportunities. (If you are not open to them, you won't even see them.) Much more vital, however, is the inner flexibility that frees us to new patterns of living, to vision in the deeper sense, to growth and change, always around an adherence to our basic principles. You need to be sure what those are, but be ready to experiment with everything else.

We need a balanced diet for the inner self—mental diet—social diet—emotional diet. We need mental, social, emotional, and spiritual ways of keeping fit. We need to get to know ourselves, which is a lifelong learning, since we keep changing.

There are not only opportunities to be seized but traps to be avoided. Over-extension is one of these, spreading ourselves too thin for our available energy. A little fatigue from brisk use of body and mind is good for us; severe fatigue is a threat and only we can know the difference. Mental entrenchment is another trap, a "digging in" that refuses to try what is new or what is going to demand something of us. Even severe frustration is a trap to be walked away from, if it can't be avoided. It is another one of those areas where a little can be stimulating but too much can be dangerous. Be aware of your needs and your wants, opportunities and temptations, callings and compulsions, and the difference.

Keep working on the development of new coping skills, new social skills. Asking for help is one of them. Everybody has to do it some time.

Living is an art, which means that the process is always more important than the product. And remember that you don't have to earn your keep.

Be aware of your gifts, and be prepared to use them, as you can, maybe in untried ways. Be aware of your pleasures, and free yourself to enjoy them.

The first thing we need from ourselves is love, and we aren't as sure to get it as one might think. Knowing how to love ourselves as our neighbors is not a common ability.

Loving anybody means allowing them their responses to stress, threat, even fatigue. We owe that to us. Given the situation most seniors live in, a certain amount of tension, even rebellion, may be necessary. We need enough acceptance to let us find what is worth rebelling against and what we can live with in peace, if not tranquillity, but adapting to a circumstance is not the same as "putting up with" it. We tend to confuse resignation with good manners, and to be concerned about "making a scene," hurting people's feelings, or losing their admiration. Resignation and acceptance are entirely different things.

Once in a while, I find myself again with a feeling of my youth, of having to fight for the value of my opinions, for the fact that what I say may be worth listening to, fighting to be me, not just a part of "they." The "they" then was the "younger generation," now it is the old one. As a categorical "they" they don't feel different.

A seventy-year-old began to see circular rainbows around oncoming lights. She blamed her car's windshield until she saw a rainbow around the moon. Her ophthalmologist diagnosed beginning cataracts, which could be corrected surgically. She asked "when?" and he said, "Not yet. For now, just enjoy your rainbows."

There are, sometimes, rainbows to enjoy, the pleasures of old age. They may seem insignificant, yet still loom large in their results, becoming ways of turning loose of anxiety and tension. Here are a few. Customize your own:

• You don't have to try every "solution" offered, because you've watched last week's magic answers become bedeviling questions.

• You can keep involvement stimulating without strain, because you've noticed that things usually improve or get worse no matter which side wins.

- You know there's at least one joker in every pack. This minimizes disillusionment.

- You're not responsible for who anybody else grows up to be. You don't have to grow up to be who anyone else wants you to.

- You don't have to have an opinion on every subject. This can make you feel so carefree you're almost dizzy.

- You can change your mind without embarrassment, having discovered that few notice when you do.

- You can wear whatever you feel in the mood to, having discovered that few notice that, either.

- When people talk about their children and grandchildren, you are pretty sure they are no closer to perfection than yours.

- You can take new directions just to see where they go.

- You can *let* things happen, without trying to make them happen.

- Every morning, you can ask, "What do I *not* have to prove today?"

- If you miss the plane, there will probably be another one; if not, you may wind up being glad of it. At worst, the odds are that the sun will rise tomorrow and rain will still sometimes make rainbows. Rainbows may show up around the moon.

For all that human life is a terminal condition, it is also a condition of blessing and mystery, usually giving more than it takes away. Those who have lived long have known that blessing and that mystery, sometimes often and well, sometimes paying too little attention. We are so painfully aware of what time takes away from us; we seldom look at what it gives.

P.S. A Word for Helping Agencies

No matter how dedicated, support organizations sometimes need to be reminded (or informed) of matters they don't always know or observe. Basic needs for support of the old include:

1. understanding what really goes on.

2. intelligent and sometimes tough concern—not just being sorry.

3. co-operation, not competition. In union may be the best answer, maybe the only answer, to knotty problems, like transportation.

4. all, but churches in particular, need to recognize the implications of this culture's nomadism. This includes the perception that past involvement in the life and work of a parish doesn't count if it wasn't done "here." In a very real sense, every local church is forced by this circumstance to offer a hit-or-miss ministry to those who are known. Finding the unknowns in a congregation can be a whole ministry in itself, not as simple or easy as bringing in new members.

We've said earlier that what most seniors need (along with others, but they urgently) is a good working philosophy of life. It seems to me that maybe churches need a bit less psychology, sociology, even gerontology!, and more energy spent in their own field of expertise: spiritual nurture, support, teaching, and therapy. Spiritual therapy? Think about it.

We all know the value of involvement, and most organizations prize it for more than altruistic reasons, since their existence depends on it. However, the subject may need more careful thought than it usually gets, especially regarding senior members. In the presence of a hard-sell insistence on working for the organization (religious or secular), those who don't feel able get pushed silently out, or just leave.

Americans don't think much of dues-paying members who do little else, but those are always needed. There is a highly judgmental factor in many organizations, where the eager and energetic insistently berate non-workers. Only the member himself can say how deep his involvement can or should go, and he shouldn't have to explain. Without that made clear, we have the "all-or-nothing" syndrome, depriving people of what could be vital but passive involvement. That is *not* an oxymoron!

One of the two most vital works of any helping group is what has come to be called consciousness-raising. The pressing problems of old age usually need ideas, concern, caring, personal action, and disseminated factual information, more than the raising or spending of money.

The other need is for stimulating motivation in the old, remembering that it is hard for the grieving or depressed to initiate anything. When old age becomes painful, beyond material relief, what is needed is nurture, guidance, stimulus, assurance that hope is possible, and just plain *caring*.

We have fought other kinds of segregation but we can easily work for the old (*for* them but not *with* them) and still leave them segregated, in a kind of benign *apartheid.* The ideal is that the old have choices, freedom to be the individuals they are, with other individuals *of all ages,* to whom they can relate as equals.

Churches and other social bodies must be sure the support they offer is not just offering solutions to problems. They must carefully listen, see truly, validate complaints, and give compassion, not pity.

We need to leave problem-solving for problems that need solving—there are plenty of those—and it is the brightest people who find that hardest to do. Many problems of old age, in it or living with it in someone else, need to be listened to, attended to, learned from, lived with, respected, wondered at, but not solved. We should reserve silence and acceptance for some things, and often awe.

Living well, at any age, is more than a problem to be solved, and possibly a skill the old can teach us.

"the best thing about leisure may be its possibility of immersing yourself . . . "

REACHING

*Once I rescued my drowning self by embracing
all my arms would hold that kept afloat —
myth and language, ways of ancient worlds,
enigma of knowledge, awe that outlives time —
looking behind the found, to find what I was.*

*I must find a further way of rescue,
not by reaching — my span and grasp are less —
but going deep into silence, into the dark
abyss like that where the stuff of world
wells up from its heart, flaming.*

*What will take me deep enough to discover,
salvage, when blood dissolves in the salt sea,
and ideas are too light, mere froth that floats?
What settles my life's foam, pierces the membranes?
Is the joy of making a way of that diving?*

"much more vital is inner flexibility . . . "

HOW FAR?

O God! How far have I to go?
        How far away I am — from me.
You I cannot escape. You are near as the going,
        though whether guide or companion or the way,
or motion itself I haven't known.

Some talk as if this were a street whereon
        we must walk, taking the right turns, with never
a signpost, never a map, and if we guess wrong
        doomed to wander always without arrival,
never to reach what we thought we traveled to.

I would not so treat an enemy, and I know
        as little of compassion as Your other creatures do.
I think there is no road — only hill, stone,
        sand shiftings that lead to desperation,
but the stars are Yours who set them, Yours is day.

I think the destination is ourselves. Our veins know
        when we turn away. We sense the right direction
by how far we are from us. It matters little in what desert
        we wander, if we are coming home. How far
I have yet to go. How far have I yet to go?

"spiritual therapy? Think about it . . . "

PRAYER FOR A CLOUD

The sky is limitless,
the ground nurtures,
but I wander without direction
a horizon that circles.

I look for more than freedom,
I need more than shelter.
Give me, Lord, a cloud to lead me
and fire to light the dark.

I know the creature that I am
but not what that may mean.
I grow and learn and diminish.
Where is the wonder?

My questions have no answers.
My answers all are empty.
I need a cloud of Your presence
and fire to light me home.

TURNING LOOSE

Holding a Tiger by the Tail

Most seniors have spent a lifetime acquiring things, which doesn't make them different from anybody else. Since they have been at it longer, their acquisitiveness has left them (us) with many things they don't have room for. If you still have a house full of furniture, knick-knacks, memorabilia, and consumer goods in general, and you've opted for smaller quarters, you may be holding a tiger by the tail. How do you turn loose?

You probably don't suddenly divorce the tiger. More likely, you finally noticed that the tiger is a tiger, and you're going to have to do something about it. You've probably done something like that before, maybe many times, especially if you've moved a lot. It's that time again, but maybe more drastic. Letting go is the work of a lifetime, and it doesn't apply only to objects.

You've probably always assumed old age was a time of cutting back, doing and having less, but it just burst out of assumption.

The Gains of Losing

Maybe the assumption that old age must be a traumatic time is also false. If subtraction is a traveling companion of old age, it sometimes turns into a friend. It does have an up side.

There may be gains in losing.

We live in a world which insists that the bluebird of happiness has its nest on the plus symbol of the calculator we measure our lives by, but the ornithology may be wrong. The bird may be extinct.

We started out with nothing: naked, hungry, powerless.

Then we began to add, to our bodies, our possessions, our influence, and however we could, our power. (Whatever else it is, the dollar is a symbol and means of power. It is one of the Great Symbols we talked about earlier.)

We seem to be animals who collect, as well as ones who make. Apparently our hands are shaped for picking things up and holding them rather than disposing of them. How we collect things! We buy in order to possess, then possess for the sake of possessing, and then we buy for the sake of buying, and collect for the sake of collecting. Addition can become addiction.

Beyond the primary needs of food, clothing, and shelter, we have a yearning, apparently a need, for something we cannot name, and we keep trying to satisfy that need with things. When we have shelter, we still keep looking for a safe place, when we have enough bread, we're still hungry.

The basic human emptiness is inner, and can't be filled by any amount of things, though Heaven knows, we try. The consumer society promises us fulfillment by acquisition, and offers us activities to distract us from the emptiness. For a while this may work, but one day we find the emptiness still there. Often, it is not until we reach seniority that we make this discovery, so we blame old age for it. The emptiness, like our shadows, has been following us all our lives.

As we diminish, the emptiness gets bigger. We've been empty ever since we were born, as we have been aging all that time, but we just recently noticed both. About the same time, we began to see practical reasons for lessening our hoard of things. Not only is the new room or apartment too small, we're getting tired, and things require caring for. They represent Responsibility.

When I moved from house to apartment, I had to dispose of most of what the house contained. It wasn't as hard to do as I had expected. There was even, along with some wistfulness, a sense of relief.

I looked to see what objects I didn't want to leave behind. The first I thought of was a palo verde tree then in bloom, entertaining hummingbirds. We had grown that tree from a seed. The second was a huachuca agave, the grace of whose growing we had watched for years.

Well, that told me I couldn't take the most important things along. But I didn't exactly leave them behind. The tree will some day be cut down, and I wouldn't want to watch that, but it was not going to live forever. Now no one can cut it out of my inner vision. If I couldn't see other trees, I would always see that one, in its growing (now taller than the house) and its golden flowering.

This turned into a continuing education. Almost every time I parted with something, I felt a new lightness, release from weight I wasn't aware of. Of course this wasn't done in the context of tragedy. I wasn't losing everything, as people do in the disasters that punctuate human experience, but I began to learn how to judge what is worth keeping and what can be left without serious regret.

Clutter as Enemy

These were not big losses (I have known those) yet who knows what is major and what is trivial under the eye of eternity? I was sifting, finding what mattered to me. This produced many surprises. The diminishing turned out to be mostly a process of uncluttering, and I know clutter to be the enemy of good art. Similarly, it is the enemy of serenity, even the enemy of memory. (I forget things worst when my thoughts are cluttered.) "Simplify, simplify," said Thoreau.

The poet's rule is "less is more." This may be true of the art of living, especially toward it's completion. I remember the man in the New Testament story, who was going to build a larger barn to hold his wealth, but died and didn't need a barn any more. I think at this stage, we don't need bigger barns.

The things I was giving up were not always clutter. Their place in my life had changed, and I had, too. I am still uncluttering my life, and in the process I find values, I discover what is essential, I know what things are not worth the space they take up, even what may have kept me from growing.

For aging is growth, though society presents it as a kind of un-growing. Sometimes that's what it is, but we may find that as our horizons narrow, our personal environment can grow invisibly rich. Society sees only the visible.

There are also treasures in our lives that can't be seen and don't need barns to hold them. The best are the invisible people we contain. We are becoming new people, but also still the ones we were. Fifteen-year-old Christine is still a part of me. I must acknowledge and honor her, along with the toddler I was, the newly-married, the mother, along also with the editor, the believer and the cynic, the dancer and the post-polio who had to learn to walk again. So, too, I am the teacher I've been, and the student I was and am, the writer and certainly the reader. These people don't take up space, and usually they don't ever become irrelevant to new phases of life. I don't have to part with them. Indeed, I can't. They belong wherever I go.

Many programs for the old are coming into being, set up by communities and fellowships and churches. Seniors are a new social concern and a whole new industry. I find myself hoping these programs won't be conducted as if their beneficiaries were a different kind of people, as if on a given birthday, we turn into a new species. Such programs, no matter how splendid, can't do all that is needed; we must, at whatever age, provide personal programs for our own aging. We are all doing it. Another word for it is living. You stop one; you stop the other.

I didn't expect it, but my move turned into an adventure. It came to feel less and less like the end of something (which it was, of course) and more and more, felt like a beginning, which it also was, and keeps on being, though yes! I sometimes forget that.

This personal divestiture is wholly different from the losses sometimes dealt out to us. Those we suffer, in both senses of the word. If your house burns down you don't have to decide what you are willing to part with. It carries little decision-making but much sorrow.

This deliberate subtracting is a matter of choice, of choice after choice, as a matter of fact, carefully undertaken. The same things may take leave of your life, however and why ever it happens. The difference is not in what is lost but in our chance to choose. What may be stolen from us isn't necessarily different from what we donate, but we are different in the doing. And the skills we learn in voluntarily turning loose can serve us if we ever have to suffer similar material losses.

In our seniority, we may gradually slide from the human need for discovery to over-emphasis on needed security, and then define security too inclusively. We still need discovery, and sometimes we make it by uncovering what has been with us all the time.

Abandoning some things only hurts because they are familiar, not because of their inherent worth. They don't need to be familiar *and comfortable* in order to be held onto with what can be literally a death-grip. No matter how painful, familiarity is itself perceived as a kind of comfort.

In the end, what you unclutter is yourself, and doing that, you become more yourself. The central you becomes more visible, at least to you. We've heard about "finding yourself" but this is more a matter of pulling yourself out of hiding. The self to be found is not static but a process, as music is process.

I said I was sifting, and this is the best description I know for this process of turning things loose. There aren't any rules to tell you what to keep and what to turn loose of. One person's treasure is another's trash, and one's clutter is another's comfort. Certainly I found that the things I needed to keep were not the ones any appraiser would have agreed to.

In fact, many of the things I needed most to keep were things that had become a part of me. Most were invisible to others, they were seldom momentous. An important one recently acquired is the visit of a hummingbird to check out the three hummers that hang in my front window, of straw and ceramic and stained glass. The visitor hovered for a while, then touched the glass in front of each one with his beak.

From long ago, there is a trout for breakfast that half an

hour before had been swimming in a mountain stream. There is a storm marching over mountains toward me, trailing rosy veils of rain, there is plainsong heard in a monastery chapel, and walking home from a date on a brick sidewalk, in jasmine-perfumed night. It would break my heart to lose those things. When I shifted my belongings, these were left for me.

I parted with heirlooms more easily, and have already given some of them to my children. But this is how my sifter worked. You will have your own, and it will measure differently.

Rituals of Goodbye

There are usually among our belongings things we keep out of a sense of loyalty, to people who gave them to us, to almost forgotten standards, to significant events, to ways of life we no longer live. Loyalty is a beautiful virtue, and it usually feels good, but loyalty lives in hearts and minds and memories, not in objects, and pain is not loyalty. Many valuable things are only valuable, only worth keeping, *in their context.*

The pain of giving things up, whether they are major or minor, can be surprisingly eased by rituals of goodbye. This is what funerals are chiefly about, and why survivors need them. This is why we have formal memorials for valuable people, even for valuable things like a demolished city, a sunken battleship. This is why monuments are still standing all over the world that were erected by forgotten people to keep other people from being forgotten.

Americans aren't much on rituals—they think! But of course we have them, like our ways of beginning things and ending them. Ritual is a basic human enterprise. Why else the national anthem to begin a baseball game, why the seventh-inning stretch? Why else special clothing? Symphony orchestras seldom perform in jeans, baseball players don't wear overalls. Ritual is the reason, but it is reason. What we wear makes a difference in us. Prescriptive dress varies widely from era to era but there are always prescriptions. The "flower children" had their uniforms.

Rituals of goodbye help to ease whatever hurt comes from turning loose. They are not, of course, logical. Living is not logical, loving is not logical, what we feel has little or nothing to do with logic. Don't try to be too consistent. You don't need a "valid" reason for a ritual. There will be reason, but you may not know it. If it isn't hurtful to anyone and the impulse is there, do it. Make monuments, not for the absent but for you.

When I walked away from what had been my house, I blew a kiss to the blooming palo verde, I saluted the agave. It helped. Never underestimate the value of a symbolic gesture.

A final thought about the exchange of house for apartment: Not-owning is a kind of freedom, though it isn't freedom from responsibility. I am in a way more responsible for how I use something when it belongs to another, but the responsibility is limited. Does this speak to my not owning the world I live in? Is my body, my mind, my influence, whatever power I have, only mine for use, perhaps, belonging to another? Some great minds and spirits have answered that with a firm "Yes."

Doing Philosophy

You don't have to answer those questions, but whatever your deepest beliefs, they are questions worth asking, and worth thinking about. I call that kind of thinking-about "doing philosophy."

Philosophy is a subject we've dealt with before. Literally, it is the love of wisdom, a subject as old as man and as necessary as your thumb. When Joseph Campbell spoke of "following your bliss" he was talking philosophy. I could wish he had used a bigger word than "bliss," which sounds misleadingly like the pursuit of feeling good. When we talk seriously about purpose, or calling, or value, or principle, we are doing philosophy.

It can take you a long way from mere good-feeling, to the immeasurable joy of fulfillment (the filling of that human emptiness) and far beyond happiness. It lives in the land that joy lives in, and love, and wonder. It may sit unused with the family Bible on a shelf somewhere, but when the little quirks of life are dislodged by things more huge than it is, we are likely to consult them both.

When I write about "calling" I am not talking about a narrow field of service, or a divine blueprint for your life, but about the breadth of life itself, and what can make it worth living. I'm writing of mystery that leads us like a light, through our dark wildernesses.

When we speak of wisdom, and of philosophy, of fulfillment and of calling, we are touching the mystery that *human* life is, indeed of the mystery that all life is. Philosophy didn't begin with the Greeks, and though it may look otherwise, it is a long way from being dead in our time. It is a concern that reaches from the sciences, which it brought into being long ago, to psychology, especially in its humanistic approaches to the ills of mind and soul, and theology, the study of the things of God, as far as we can perceive them.

Philosophy is how to face the universe in wonder, how to relate to your lovers and your enemies, and how to stay honest, and why. It is ethics and morality, inner light and inner guidance, the Golden Rule and the practicality that knows what will work and what won't. Philosophy's school meets in the days of a life, which is why old age is supposed to be a time of wisdom.

The familiar "serenity prayer" asks for serenity to accept the things we cannot change, courage to change the things we can, and *wisdom to know the difference.* This is probably as good a definition of wisdom as you're likely to find.

It's not a kind of knowledge, but a kind of exploration, all the way from how our minds, hearts, and wills work to our relationship with the Mystery behind and beyond and beneath all mysteries, including the mystery we are.

When it is time to judge what to keep and what to turn loose, philosophy is the only reliable guide. Its guidance will be in asking questions, not delivering answers.

The Artist's Daring

This process of turning loose is creative, and valuable beyond the immediate and the obvious. It is, in its own way, a work of making, as well as the work of ceasing to have.

Human creativity is not limited to artists. All of us are given that ability. Of course, it is only God who can create *ex nihilo* (from nothingness, which is what "chaos" means). He can make something come into being for the first time; what we do is to make a new thing out of shattered pieces of an old one—if we are willing to shatter it. That part is frightening, giving up what is, in order to make real what is to be. Artists through the ages have told us it is this destruction, this made absence, that most requires the courage to create.

The moment of the artist's daring is when he faces the blank canvas, the silence of unmade music, his still body. That is when she is impelled to fill what is empty, it is when he must put onto canvas color from his mind and hand, when she must carve from formlessness the form she feels. It is when the writer must put words to the unmarked sheet of paper, as they are heard not yet spoken.

Only artists? Are we not all called to be artists in the creating and shaping, the singing and saying of the life we are given? The requirements are the same. As the artist must continually move away from the made thing, out to the nothingness that calls forth a new making, we are all led away from the life we have carved or sung, to fill another emptiness with what is yet to be. We have to turn loose, that we may again hold, and we do it as long as we live.

We make and we re-make, not correcting errors but re-writing in the way the author does, smoothing and polishing in the way of the craftsman. When it becomes vital for you to turn loose things tangible or intangible, this may be a calling to re-make the singular person that is your art, that is yourself. To have room for this, you may have to give up something, to turn loose, and face your version of the block of stone, the blank paper, the silent instrument.

The calling may be to patient excision of all that clutters. That is the price of excellence, in a work of art or in a life.

It can be frightening, but it's one of the most exciting things that can happen to you, and it will keep on happening, if you are willing to let go the tiger's tail and risk his claws.

No one, not even God, will do it for you. He has given the material, the ability, and the calling (the command/urge) to create, and not just once, but to do it over and again as long as you breathe again, as long as you waken new each day. The material is your own life, the making is many things in one: it is an obedience, it is adventure, it is daring, it is purpose, it is the height of art, it is the loving act of the child of God who, in making, is the living image of the Maker.

"in the end, what you unclutter is yourself . . . "

MAYBE

I would know more in the mode of music
I cannot hold, except as it echoes
in my inner ear, delicately balanced.
I would know more in the mode of poetry
I can be held by, moved, finding
in the old new things, matrix where words
crystallize in new-created shapes.

Maybe living with absence can produce
presence, like that of an absent David
whose voice I have heard in psalms,
those ardent allelulias in the dark,
an absent Moses speaking in stone words,
a Prometheus, an Oedipus, a Lear
—old acquaintance, lately ripened.

Perhaps if I can hold desires virgin
I will have all that I need, and if I learn
to possess what I cannot own I will
no longer by possessed by things,
if I treasure what's done I can stop
urgently doing, let clasped things
fall from my hands, not in sorrow.

If I walk the world in wonder, claiming kin
without claiming, I may someday consent
to relinquish it. I am finding
surfeit spills over in loss but
every emptiness is filled. Maybe
in this time of losing and being found
I can be filled with waiting emptiness.

"we make a new thing, out of shattered pieces of the old . . . "

NEW FIRE

I am growing colder
where has gone the heat of making's fervor

a candle quenched by fitful winds
blowing down the corridor of years
or have I burned it through the night
to see what are dreams men call reality
while the real awaits in dark
for which I foolish virgin
have no light left

is there flint in old bones
steel in a weathered will

can I strike them to light new fire
on some paschal wick — ner pesach *— or*
scant kindling laid in a hearth
that age may be if I learn
not to covet the sun

ner pesach—Passover light

"there may be gains in losing . . . "

TIME THE WINNOWER

Some of the rules have been rescinded
but the training functions.
Some of the beauties are tattered now
but beauty is not fragile.
Some loves are lost and friends vanished
but loving continues.

Time, like a wind, melts snow to water,
thins imprisoning ice
or blows afar the cruel sand
forbidding the first blade.
Like wind it can uncover seeds, to die,
or to sprout with promise of bread.

The grain of harvest
lies on the threshing floor, waiting
to be relieved of its chaff.
Mere clutter clutching attention
muffles passion, but time's wind
blows away light things.

Its force rising, it may bare
what frantic days covered with duties
and fears, littered with idle wishes,
shredded intentions. This wind may tear
away white flags. Purpose can ride
this wind, and simplify.

Time bends passion doesn't blow it away.
When pain has healed, its fever
may breathe warmth into stillness.
When fires burn down
their embers can still kindle
to destroy, or to bring light.

MAKING A LIFE

No Right Way

There is no one right way to age, but there are some that bear thinking about. This is a time to choose what we do and avoid on the basis of our preferences rather than the "shoulds" we once lived by. Even if those "shoulds" were valid, they may not be now. We need, perhaps, to find out which "shoulds" still matter. They may be fewer than you think.

None of life's gifts carries a guarantee; most carry responsibilities. The responsibilities of youth are largely to your own future; the responsibilities of the middle years are largely to other people; the responsibilities of old age are primarily to yourself. It is probably one of the chief duties of old age to give up most of the earlier ones.

As we've kept saying, old age is not a pathologic condition, though cosmetic ads and fitness magazines talk as if it were, and their products could cure it. There is no more a way to cure old age than to cure adolescence. There are a few ways to prevent old age: drinking while driving comes to mind.

What we need is not a way to cure old age but to use it skillfully and, if possible, enjoyably. It furnishes its own tools: your experience, your abilities—mental, emotional, and spiritual. If there were ever a do-it-yourself project, this is it. If you include the grace of God, and your asking for it.

Questions to Ask

At the threshold of this section of our lives, we have questions to ask: How can we live with our particular surroundings humanely, in dignity and humor, in acceptance and (yes) rebellion, in anguish and (surprisingly, sometimes) joy? Most important, how can we live with them in honor? These are matters of survival. The answers are for the making of a life.

Old age once was being "turned out to pasture," nothing more expected or allowed. Now we are told to be active, but I'm not sure how "active" is defined. If it means serve on more committees, do more volunteer work, travel farther, I must say "no, thank you," but I don't want to graze pasture, either.

Since age is often equated with disability and youth with action, some of the activity going on in old people is only a desperate kind of running-in-place, to prove they are not losing ground, but it doesn't prove anything of the sort.

I've done volunteer work, and it was rewarding. I recommend it, wholeheartedly, but what you choose doesn't have to be altruistic to be worth doing. I've served on the committees. Now I'd like to do things I wanted to but didn't have time for before (sometimes because of too many committees).

I'm finding that my body can't keep going quite as long in a day as it used to, but my head and heart can feel unemployed.

The maturity business entertains us. People point out jobs that need doing. There's a gap between these and I think I fell in it. I don't want ways to fill (or kill?) time. Is my time no more important than that to anybody, even me? Do I still have to justify my existence? Or may this be a time to involve myself in something for sheer pleasure, maybe begin a whole new career? Why not? Here is an emptiness I didn't have time to notice before. What am I looking for?

What men and women are really seeking, say some wise thinkers like Viktor Frankl, Rollo May, and Abraham Maslow, is *meaning*. This, they say, is the thing without which life becomes "stale, flat and unprofitable." I'm not sure precisely what "meaning" means but I know what they're talking about.

It is in old age that this search can be intensified, broadened, and/or focused, but it seems to me that all too often, it is merely given up. Resignation may pass for serenity, but that isn't what it is. Meaning is a basic need, like food and air. To resign oneself to a lack of it is to give up on living.

Such "meaning" is not found just in understanding how things work (though curiosity can be a first step), or in amassed knowledge, or in ideas, but these are all functions of the mind that searches. "Meaning" is not wholly intellectual or emotional.

In the Nazi concentration camps, Dr. Frankl noted how those who had some kind of meaning in their lives survived incredibly, when those who lacked it succumbed. He said that without a sense of meaning, men and women fall into despair. Joseph Campbell put it that we need to find things that feel worthwhile, that make sense out of life. The basic question about life isn't: What does it mean? but, Is there meaning in it? What we need is a "yes" to that, not an explanation.

Meaning is not the same as a "purpose in life," but close. At least purpose, serious or not, can lend meaning when intellect can conceive of none. What we intend by "meaning" is very real but mystery—not puzzle, but depth. It is such mystery as all philosophic systems and great religions address, and, rightly or wrongly from other viewpoints, is the source of their power.

I want to enrich this gift of time, but I'm not talking about always taking life solemnly. Work and play aren't antithetical. Both are too valuable to be used just for filling up time. Americans sometimes have trouble understanding that while fun can be work (we know that—so many of us work at recreation), work can be fun, often more fun than anything else in the world.

Artists know the work that matters to you is pleasure and the joy of your art demands hard work. I found out long ago that you don't get much out of what you don't put much of yourself into.

Perhaps what I want is enterprise that deserves emotional energy, intense caring. I'm talking about things that matter to *me,* things I'm curious about, or have wished I could explore, back when I was spending all that time and energy on necessities.

I'd also like to find people with whom I can share my enthusiasms, my curiosity, my discovery. I want to share the adventure of learning.

Back when communities tended to stay put, people grew up

knowing one another's viewpoints, concerns, interests. In this nomadic society, we lack ways of finding others who are curious about what we wonder about, who care about what we care about, who speak our language. Maybe this aspect of our nomadic life is a big source of loneliness and depression, in people of all ages.

Wants and Needs

With more time and less energy, I need to find out what I really want, what I feel I'm missing, what can fill that gap. I remember Itzhak Perlman saying that "you have to separate your abilities from your disabilities." Maybe that's a good place to begin. Never mind what I can't do and what I can't have. What are my abilities? my possibilities?

He also said "you can no longer afford partial attention."

I suspect one of my first needs is from myself, to lighten the demands I put on me, and to give myself permission to be odd, to non-conform, to fail, and to succeed. I need to give total attention, even to myself.

I know I need balance. Now that multiple demands of a busy life don't furnish it, I need consciously to work toward balance. I need mental work, to keep the equipment functioning if nothing else. It's pleasure, too, one many people forget and some are afraid of, as others fear flying, or heights, or deep water.

I need emotional connections, happenings. Is there such a thing as emotional work? I think there may be, and that some of us are afraid of that, as others are afraid of the mental kind. Have I been neglecting it? I need to respond to the emotional in the arts and to cultivate my own emotional garden of personal encounters. It isn't just a flower garden; it offers food.

I need physical rest, exercise, nourishment. I've probably been over-providing the last but neglecting the first two.

I need spiritual stimulus, exercise and nourishment, as well, alone and with others. Whatever my religious beliefs or doubts, I may be letting compassion and meditation wither, forgetting the deepest needs, my relationship with God, my life of prayer.

I may even have said prayers and gone to church, but not taken these deep enough. More vital and more constant than saying prayers is the need of prayer as listening, a kind of attention, a deliberately chosen vulnerability to the divine, in me and beyond me. It is only this kind of acceptingness that can help me loosen attempts to control, while staying responsible for myself.

It is only this kind of receptiveness that can keep sweet and wholesome and uncluttered my interactions with others, avoiding manipulation and the complications of envy and covetousness, of competition and misunderstanding.

This is the heart of intercession, the prayer for others. We don't need to instruct God about their needs (he knows, or he isn't God) or even to ask blessing for them. The basis of this kind of prayer is self-giving and turning loose, giving our concern for them to God, to use as he will, giving up our certainties, handing over our bewilderments. We offer this kind of prayer with respect for the autonomy of those we pray for and for God who knows them better than we do.

Intercessory prayer is vital to relationship; too often instead of praying *for* people, we only pray *about* them.

Intercession's self-giving requires readiness possibly (but not necessarily) to be instruments of God's answers. The most urgent needs of those we pray for are the same as our own: need to be seen as unique persons, to be heard rightly and with respect, and need for communion, with nature, with God, and with one another. We pray in the context of their humanity and our own, not deploring it but giving thanks for it.

Old age is the means and the need to work toward the fullness of that humanity. Keeping bodies and minds functioning is only part it. Wholeness requires health also in the realm of the spirit. "Spirituality" is more than "religion," more than morality or ethics, though they arise from our spirituality and their quality is determined by it.

Send your spiritual life deep now, make it more personal, unique to yourself, rather than only the keeping of institutional codes, as valuable as those are. Old age can set you to finding and developing your own gifts of the spirit, to hearing and answering your own true callings. Here is found fulfillment.

Your world can some time shrink, to the limit of a room, a chair, a bed, but the world of your attention may keep on expanding. For this, there are no limits beyond those of life itself and your ability to take command of who you are. We may not be able to do all we want to, but we need all our abilities. You can't afford partial attention. You need your whole life. Claim it.

Structure and Freedom

Did you ever notice how days in a hospital seem to revolve around mealtimes, though the meals are seldom worth waiting for? Once I found a better way.

I made a structure for the time, allotting periods for reading, letter-writing, meditation, knowing there would be interruptions, but hoping by lunch to feel I had accomplished something. Lunch came around sooner.

Being a hospital patient is in some ways a kind of prison sentence; in others it is sheer freedom, for your usual duties are abrogated. Medical procedures are only interruptions. Because I was ill, I had to keep things undemanding, but I had a structure. It altered the whole experience, somehow. I didn't have to decide when to start or stop anything,

I didn't have to be "in the mood" to do something. In hospital, one is so seldom in the mood for undertaking anything. I tapered off the energy requirements as the day wore on, with needlework and listening to music. Later, I was able to add short walks.

During most of my life, I've had to do the opposite, to insert freedom into the duties, arrange for occasional "time off." Without that, I would have lost the zest of everything.

What reminded me of that hospital time was reading a book

about the poet Louise Bogan, in which the author referred to "the structuring of the days to circumvent despair." After Edward's death, when time seemed a vast landscape around me, I again found structure useful. I scheduled time at the typewriter, tending the garden, writing letters, getting out of the house to do errands and enlarge my horizon. It was a way to get through a time that seemed endless, a way of "circumventing despair."

I think this twinned need for alternate effort and rest is basic to human life. It probably was what God had in mind when he instituted the Sabbath, the "time off" *par excellence* (though the Sabbath has sometimes been made less restful than any labor).

This pulse, this pattern of ebb and flow, is fundamental to the creative life. The arts show us freedom as necessary for the art to be envisioned, but structure to give it form, reality. The Greeks knew it as the work of Apollo, god of order and harmony, and Dionysus, god of the unconscious, inebriation, and passion. Apollo ordered, Dionysus unearthed and kindled. Good art demands respect be paid to both forces.

I have to write that way. I must first let unconscious or semiconscious forces flow where they take me. Then I must find the order that imposes itself on the work. Finally I rewrite, drawing alternately on both currents, in order to enflesh that living skeleton art must have, however invisible in the product.

Total freedom, of course, doesn't exist for us, but even excessive freedom leads to nothing brought into being, in a life or in a studio. It banishes Apollo. Total structure is also impossible, but the over-structured life fetters spontaneity and wit, binding Dionysus, stiffening the resilience necessary to the mystery of creating or the mystery of living.

We human beings are complex organisms, operating (physically or otherwise) by balancing divergencies. We get in trouble when we let one tendency thwart its opposite. Yet this is what we tend to do. The rigid person can stiffen with advancing time, losing capacity for change and for seizing opportunity. The flexible person may bog down in a morass of indecision, his potentialities stifled. Even growth, when unlimited, turns dangerous.

A metaphor for this, in art or in life, is found in our own bodies. A skeleton is inflexible bones, jointed but unmoving. Muscles which move must attach to rigid bones, or they can only quiver ineffectually.

Think of it this way:

> *A skeleton never went anywhere*
> *by itself. But muscles without bones*
> *are blobs. Rigidity comes with death,*
> *identifies it, following flaccidity,*
> *death's other self.*
> > *Life*
> > *balances*

.

To create a work of art, you must alternate structure and freedom, emotional dynamic and mental skills. To be truly alive, at any age, you must balance freedom with structure, strength with flexibility. "Here I stand" demands "Here I go," and *vice versa*.

This Is Later

If you wait too long for the "right time" to do things, you can wait right on into the impossible time.

You wait for the time when everything important is done, when you get your degree, the mortgage is paid off, you get over the grief, you retire. You wait until the children are self-sufficient, educated, and/or safe, until the children are mature. It's your own maturity must tell you your right time, not theirs.

The children may never seem mature to you, any more than you did to your parents. Their education, please God, will never be finished. Unfortunately, they will never be safe.

We can wait, in short, until everything in our lives is out of the way, until all responsibilities, even all projects, are finished. By then we may be finished. If you are ever to paint, or go to Tibet, or take up tatting; if you are ever to learn to pray or love or forgive, you must begin now.

Writing is what I know about. I have begun doing it, over and again throughout my life, because I kept putting it aside, usually for what I thought duty demanded. Some of the duties weren't really duties, and some nobody ever seemed to know I did. Even if you began, then lost momentum or forgot your purpose, you can still do it. Last Wednesday might have been a better time, but you can't begin last Wednesday. Begin now.

It may be easier when you're older, when you don't have to explain what you are doing, and you can risk failure, since nobody is watching that closely. (This is the up side of "nobody cares.") When you are old, you don't have to find something to write about that nobody else has written, something to paint that nobody else has painted. You always write or paint or make music about you, anyway, and now there is so much of you. You have so much of a life stored in your head and your heart and your body, accessible only to you, and always there.

The young don't have all that life stored, no matter how much vitality they do have. There are so many things they haven't tried yet, so many directions they haven't taken. There is so much history that, for them, is buried in books but for us is alive. They haven't had time to train their minds to daydream and their imagination to lift off. They've had too little practice in recognizing themselves. Their failures are so dishearteningly fresh, while ours are old familiars. They haven't known as many people, gone as many places, lived in as many emotions and events. Their advantage is that all these lie ahead; ours is that we've done them.

At any time, the path you travel may be in bad repair. You fall into potholes, trip over rocks and hummocks. Sometimes you find that a storm has downed a great tree, and you must climb laboriously over it, getting scratched and bruised. You may have to stop a bit, to recover strength and direction.

And sense of purpose, which may be the last thing you get back. It is what you need most, however vague your definition of it. It isn't the purpose itself that matters, but your *sense of purpose*. When you regain that, you can pick yourself up, dust the dirt off your hands*, and—

Begin now. You can't do it any younger, though maybe you should have; you may not get a chance later. But that is not because of being the age you are. It was always true.

You deserve whatever it was you were putting off to do. All too often, two of you were waiting to do it together "later" and now there is only one. Maybe you still can do it. If so, it will have a poignancy that is not the celebration you envisioned but may be a treasure all the same. Or maybe you can do something now that is like what you had in mind. When you do it, it may feel like keeping a promise.

I remember lunching with a lovely lady who had just moved from her house into a small apartment. She wondered what to do with the "good" china she was packing to store away. Her daughters had their own. I said, "Use it."

This is one of the compensating pleasures that may walk hand-in-hand with the losing. You don't always have to give up the beautiful and keep the practical. Meals served on the best plates taste better than those on the every-day ones. Eating by yourself is one of the dimmer prospects of being alone. Do anything you can to make it better.

I said, "Give away the plastic dishes. There are people who need them. You saved the best china for later. This is later."

We save things—for what? for when? to be seen by whom? In uncluttering your closets and your life, remember you are worth the "good things." So wear your best clothes, even if you're not going to see anybody unusual. You have a mirror. We wait until some things stop being possible and others fade or crack. It's important to know when "later" gets here.

Keep the delicate furniture, get out the heirlooms, buy some flowers. Use things you've saved for special occasions. Believe me, this is a special occasion.

Which leads somehow to the subject of giving, not to your grandchildren (you know how to do that) but to *you*. As there

*This is similar to what the Bible means by "shook off the dust [of a place] from their feet."

were pleasures you waited for, there are gifts you wished somebody would give you. Give them to yourself. If they are what you really want, this will work well, once you get used to it. If the real want was to be paid attention to, thought about, you can do that, too. It won't be the same, but it, too, can be surprisingly good. The possible is the better part of wisdom.

Though a legendary gift of old age, wisdom is not automatic. It is a gift, the same way a talent is a gift, probably more rare than most talents. If you are willing to look bravely back at your failures as well as your successes, your wanderings as well as your arrivings, you may find you have gotten wisdom.

However, your own corner of the world may not recognize its need or your gift; what is important is that you do. You cultivate wisdom in the field of your own living. You exhibit it best in the way you treat yourself. This is the pattern not only for wisdom but for healthy spirituality, for moral fiber. It is the life-wide pattern of health and growth: our care begins with us, but when healthy it doesn't stop there.

Your biggest present responsibility may be simply that of really *living*, and letting others see it happen. Human beings need all the help they can get in learning how to live humanly. Especially they need demonstrations, examples. Those who are struggling with mid-life's "dailyness" may get glimpses of freedom from those who have made it through to the next stage, but only from those who are free. The duty of living fully is first a duty to you, to accept your own worth, your own significance. That is the context in which old lives can show wisdom to younger ones.

Maybe the achievement of old age *is* a talent, to be worked at, its crafts learned, energy invested in it, its existence rejoiced in, before its wonders can be offered to the world.

A Short Life

Relatively speaking, you've lived a long time but it doesn't always feel that way. Sometimes it seems to be such a short life, set in mountains and trees and rocks that last longer. What can you do with a short life? What can you make of it?

Consider the long majestic march of history, plus all that time before anything was written. Some of the stones men and women carved and fitted still stand. Names borne by the stones are muttered echoes of older ones. Terrible deeds have been done, but so have wonderful deeds, done by men and women whose lives were no longer than yours, many whose scope was much shorter.

The gift of old age is the gift of humanity, probably not the highest state of being, but possibly the most mysterious, the least understood, especially by those who possess it. What is expected of us? We really don't know. We don't know what to expect of ourselves.

The gift is being the person you are. Make the most of it. The gift is living when you do. Don't take it lightly. Sometimes we claim to be created by circumstances, but that isn't wholly true. Sometimes we claim to be created by our heritage, but this, also, can't be wholly true.

In spite of nature and nurture, we are collaborators in the making of ourselves, not creators of life but artists of the shaping of it, committed to a work of genius and dedication. Your old age is the consistency and pliability of the material you have to work with today. See what you can make of it.

Whatever the intention for the work, the first aim of every artist is the joy of the making. May yours be that joy, in every age of your life. I can wish you no better.

"the gift of old age is the gift of humanity . . . "

SUMMER LIGHT

The slanting light snags on the saguaros
polishes satin of poppies
paints the sky
making it absorbent to the songs
of mockingbirds and finches.

Noon is uncaring and violent but morning
lustily young is ready to promise
anything. Evening takes away time, ready
to forgive everything.

"your biggest . . . responsibility may be that of really living . . ."

I, COLUMBUS

I have discovered in my life uncharted continents
great rocklands and even tropic oceans peopled
— peopled, but by whom? — a world
where even the law of gravity has not yet
been enacted and where the nursery rules
have all grown up, a world where reason
is ever unreasonable and never sweet.
   I have found deserts, archipelagos
   where common sense does not make sense
   but where the senses thrive, junglish.

This is not the golden country I set out for
not the India of spices
but a spicy fruit of a planet.
Nor is this the jewel-set terra that we find
when we first learn to open our eyes
(and lose when we learn to close them)
— that was discovery enough — but this
is a whole whirling jewel of itself.
   Dreams may have lands like that in them
   and dreams are not confined to sleep
   but this is no dream. This
   is a long awaited waking.

"there is no one right way to age . . . "

VERTIGO

Remembering and forgetting require the labor of sorting.
What is important I've never been totally sure of,
nor what is real. Is what looks false the true,
what seems unfathomable the trivial?

Maturing can make you dizzy. It isn't steady.
I develop in segments, in sections, in systems.
My life swirls out in storm cells, in hurricanes,
contracts to a cry, a flash, a recognition.

"There is another kind of memory . . . close to wonder, amazement, eagerness. "

ANAMNESIS
(Re-calling)

> *We worry about forgetting a name,*
> *losing knowledge.*
> *We should worry when we forget*
> *our sensing of what is nameless,*
> *when we lose touch with One whose name*
> *is not to be spoken lightly.*

BEACHCOMBING

This section I call "Beachcombing" because it gathers the
figures and ideas and questions cast up by preceding chapters,
and it is, even in its shift from prose to poetry, a figure for the
changed environment of old age. Objects are revealed by the
ebbing tide, some we thought we had lost, some we never knew
we had, some of them broken, some beautiful.

This chapter plays the instrument of poetry, traditional
accompaniment for longings and discoveries. Its lullabies and
elegies, its celebrations are the music of this time, though we
first sang them long ago.

Those singing years usually had little attention for intan-
gibles. Subtly and secretly, our importances have rearranged
themselves.

Stroll along this beach, gather what is interesting, or

curious, or beautiful, what starts a dream or asks further thought. Please come back here from time to time. It will not have changed, but you may have.

When I want to think, I read and write prose. When I want to feel my way deeply into something, I turn to poetry—mine and that of others. Over thousands of years, poetry has played literary music that men and women found delight and healing in. Our culture knows it only slightly, and needs more of it. Some poetry, like a sea-shell, sings to itself music of the world's restless waters, and if you listen receivingly, you will hear it.

So we return to the extended metaphor of old age as life's ebbing tide. The book which began with facts and discussion has done its own flowing. Like a human life, as it ebbs it cherishes the sensory (even when senses are blunted), it trusts what is felt more than what is learned, it concentrates on hope rather than wishes, on love (even love lost) rather than desire.

On your own beach, you will likely find more regrets for possibilities missed than for acts committed. We have all done things we ought not to have done, but we have also left undone things that our lives, and maybe other lives, would have been the richer for. These are not only saintly acts omitted, good deeds neglected, and gifts ungiven. They are missed opportunities for pleasure and laughter and touching. Somewhere in the Talmud, I'm told, it is written that we shall be called to account for the permitted pleasures we have denied ourselves.

Like the tides, directed from beyond our planet-home, the out-flowing currents of a human life are revealing. Ebb tides leave behind foundations of demolished structures, litter of distant wreckage, valuable objects that don't matter any more, along with present beauty, delight, curiosity. There are horse-shoe crabs (those still-living fossils), starfishes, driftwood carved and colored by artistry of time and weather, and singing shells which once housed our fellow dwellers of earth.

Bequests of an ebbing tide seem to be largely organic, life-related, often life-enriching, life-lightening, human matters.

194

THE POEMS

ANGLES OF REFRACTION

We see the stars from dragon-guarded granite
and cannot otherwise, ever. If
we are lucky, we see dragons
by starlight.

We see worm-guarded earth from over
and cannot otherwise, until too late. If
unlucky we see earth breeding flies
and dragons.

If we let dreams hatch creatures breathing fire,
by that light we see the invisible —
strong dragons in dark skies, in daylight hovering
delicate dragonflies.

ARABESQUE

The solar system swirls, the seasons ride circus horses,
light and dark revolve as the round sun whirls the hour.
Platforms of granite slide their ancient courses;
civilizations wait their turns to tower.

Every ending coils into beginning
and offers promise ranging wide and far
but progress often turns out to be spinning
us back again to where we always were.

Sometimes the trailing rutted track
almost forgot, left long ago behind
may be the way ahead, for doubling back,
the way we lost may be the one we find.

The rings of orbits link without release.
Seeds burst, to spear from leaf to bud to seed.
The maypole dance of generations does not cease;
life itself is a helix double-keyed.

My hopes twist, and my terrors,
in attempted circumventions.
My understanding mirrors
my meandering intentions.

I know that matter is but unseen motion
more reel than real, more dance than density.
Tides will girdle land as well as ocean.
All things leap through a loop we cannot see,

until the sages' tangent leads to question:
Do circles pull us downward as they spin,
wind out to a nothing that we cannot vision,
or — hint of hope — may some wind up and in

to what is beyond our dreaming and our power?

THE BEST VALENTINES

The best valentines, like the best wines
begin in earth, at the sun's warm invitation,
the sometimes cold rain needed
to deepen root. They reach to light, burgeon.
They bloom and fruit.

They never stay green tendrils, frail shoots.
Even sweet globes of passion ripened
are trodden by circumstance to burst the skins,
put to ferment by the yeast of years
to oldest magic.

They undergo long storage in a dusky dark,
ruined but becoming, changing at time's touch.
The best valentines are long distilled
of want and longing, decanted in fulfillment
that makes mere sweetness childish.

The best valentines
are red, not of summer's roses
or children's peppermints,
but wine like unmelting rubies,
priceless, beautiful.

DRAIN

I keep swimming as hard as I can in these circles because
I'm surrounded by things that are swirling away down the drain,
gurgling and furling away in a hurry to exit.
Swimming upstream from extinction I find is exhausting.

All my legs pumping, all eight of them work, like the spider
in the emptying sink, who doesn't know water twirls clockwise
in this hemisphere, does not even know what the drain is.
But then I don't either.

Heraclitus was certainly right, that everything flows,
but he didn't say, what is equally true, that things wheel,
they eddy, wind, spiral, loop, twist, and always downhill.
Which may be why I am dizzy.

I don't have to look forward in order to see things are going.
They vanish beside me, across the drain we coil down to.
They vanish behind me. New flotsam appears while I look
for old things I wasn't enough acquainted with yet.

Everything slides down the drain, even mountains pour downhill
and twine muddy arcs in the process, screwing their way
toward some drain in the ocean, some funnel in time
that sucks down the peaks and washes away all the trees.

So I keep eight legs going, but still I keep swooping on down
in the circles that take me, no matter how hard I may swim,
toward the vortex in time, the drain in the sink of the world
the gurge that everything sooner or later spins into.

EVERY LEAVE-TAKING

Every leave-taking is also an embarking.
Every journey's end begins a journey
but morning's glow can dim by sunset's tears
into false dawn that lights but grief and fears.
Birth and death men share with all earth's children.
This unknown, this veiled and delphic promise
disturbs and calms only the human years.

FORESIGHT

Sometimes I think almost as much
about death as life, and both as mystery
inevitable as autumn, intangible as space,
as present as pain. Death, like birth, is violent
wresting of gifted body into question.

I cry at threat of losing what
I don't possess — not songs of summer
but song itself, not air but light,
taste, and scent and texture —
not senses but the wealth they give to me.

Love may be at death but left awhile
to find more fully at the feet of Love,
but what of the gifts of the makers,
of wonder uncontrived, as if Beethoven
never wrote but found, and his silence caught?

Are sounds interred forever with the ears
that opened to them? Is color lost with eyes?
Or was that music echo from beyond,
escaped like shafts of light from a door ajar?
Is glory hint that I shall only leave
music and color but to be found by them?

FOR NOW

This is now.
I don't know what is next week.
Next year.
Three centuries from now.

They will come, and perhaps with more shock,
or less,
than this time has for me.
I may, or may not, see them.
I don't know.
Time was, I would have asked questions.

Now I use the time to lick whatever wounds
have been inflicted,
to recognize fatigue,
perhaps a kind of defeat,
and find I still believe in risking,
rather than safety
in human matters.

INEVITABLE ACCIDENT

"for every man, his death is an accident . . . "

Death is abstraction until it becomes
particular, then never again
it disappears, at least from dreams.
It lurks in every shadow, sometimes
it beckons to darkness seeming
just then, brighter than life.

Death is the oldest enemy,
the oldest friend. It was death
that led the way out of Eden, that
barred the gate, and always does.
It may lead onward but
it never turns back.

I have seen death be mystery
in a bloody carapace, by a roadside.
I have seen death blaze the sky
lighting a world with horror and
identification, bringing us
out of the flame, heroes.

But I have seen death be nurse
soothing the sobbing child at last
to sleep. I have seen death tidying
the toys that had lost their love.
I have seen death be guide, leading
through wonders, to destination.

LATE LESSON

In a healthy fear of dragons there's survival.
In a healthy awe of God there is delight.
But cringe too long at dragons
and you're terrified of cows
and finally go hungry all your days.
Cringe before God and you run from life himself
and the only place to run is into death.

A LONG TIME LATER

Is it time
to go back to woods in which I used to lose
myself long ago? "That was in another country"
but the wench is not dead. I am still
the loser, at least the one who can lose
myself, accidentally. Or on purpose.

The woods
are wider, but for all the pathways I run down
for certain distances, to other pathways, and
on these to others, losing myself
more seriously now . . . I think the woods
have still the same trees.

The same stars
are visible through branches
grown heavier. The trees are taller
and roots more intricately twined
but being lost among them is
a way of coming home.

Wandering around
in this wood is a way of being still.
Being alone in it is being once again
where I was before, and the small fright
is comfortably familiar, like the sigh of wind
in eaves long lived under.

The leaves sing
songs that ring true, though I can't
make out the words. The music
haunts me like one cry in a stillness.
No matter how faint or far away,
it is never trivial.

THE ONLY GAME IN TOWN

Every poet's theme is time, whatever his subject.
Love is an art as temporal as music. Nature
is that great dial whose hands spin with the planet.
Death is we know not whether a hand
turns over the hourglass.

Civilization only uses
digital figures replacing the spinning hands
but time passes, square numbers flickering
inexorable count-down. Men and women are
the only animals who count time while they dance.
In the end, time counts them into place.

SONORA

This place —
this bare place whose thorns gleam unashamed
under an ardent sun, this place
exposed and forbidding to those whose loves
beckon under soft light, with hooded eyes,
to those who prefer beauty delicate,
adorned, submissive —

this desert
is a woman naked, in her hands only
adaptations to thirst and burning,
small daggers against a golden horde,
honesty that leaves her vulnerable
to towers of glass, steel teeth, careless dreams,
to death hidden in concrete coffins.

(A young friend asked me to include this poem in the book. I wrote it about the
vulnerable desert I live in, but hers was a vision of her own old age.)

204

THE SWORD-BARRED GATE

I can't go back again to any place. This journey
onwards only. Not that places change much
in the time of this flesh. Their burning
is much slower.

> *The sea, never the same, seems changeless.*
> *Mountains rise by too much majesty*
> *for anyone to see but only angels.*
> *Deserts bloom and burn in iambic meter*
> *of the planet's poetry. I am the one*
> *who must turn to the next stanza.*

> *The sky remains, no roof but exposure.*
> *The bird who flies it beats his wings*
> *like last year's. The lizard on the rock*
> *is hard to tell from lizards running rocks*
> *before we were. It is I who am pushed*
> *into tomorrow before I taste today.*

I am hardly descendant of myself.
I keep running, still running from
the headlong start of my rough shove
into light that measures days, years.

> *And every day I am a mutant.*

I can't go back again to anywhere.
Backward searching sees with other eyes.
My eyes have sometimes died,
mummies, mocking appearances.

> *These eyes are transplants.*

> *Turning back undoes gravity, reverses*
> *the orbits of planets. It is against the law*
> *of our life, that goes from question to question*
> *in one direction. Remembering can be a toy*
> *carried in my pocket, a golden locket,*
> *a staff in my hand for rough places,*
> *or the hard husk of me, carried on my back.*

TO EDWARD, YEARS AFTER

You are no ghost. They are
   the unresting dead, the empty.
You have long come to what you always
   longed for, sometimes looked for,
though you had a life-long love affair
   with this pulsing planet.

Ghosts are the unsatisfied. The world
   is peopled with them, flesh and spirit
wandering, without compass, without star,
   without quest, without desire.
You followed some star. I could almost see
   its gleam lighting your way.

No ghost, you walk by its light yet
   places we knew, those I discover.
The voice I listen for you have lost,
   lost are the arms that embraced me,
but you speak, and from beyond time
   to time, embrace.

TOWARD CALM

Toward calm? They tell me this is time
to ease to final quiet,
as do all earthly things.
The earth of me consents. But I yet
search for what I never lost,
look to horizon, test the wind.

> *Even earth is not so still as she appears,*
> *her discontent hidden under mountains*
> *her restlessness deep fire and long time.*

Toward calm? Yes, I hope for that,
but qualified. May it be a sea calm,
surge gone deep, but not gone,
still surface only still
compared to storms. Send me
a sea calm to cradle in, rocking.

TWO

In dire times
the wondrous-wide world is able to contract,
reduce plurality to an ultimate, fragments to whole
beyond vision. Beings vanish, doings cease, leaving

> *this NOW too vast to reach beyond, to go around,*

> *this instant too transient to exist*
> *yet essence of existence*
> *flutter of reality, mere repeat*
> *of all past flutterings*

> *blaze whose fire consumes all else*
> *(itself burnt before I can say that)*

> *blotting out of earth and sky, time's trap,*
> *prison of memory and hope*

> *itself beyond measure, ephemeral yet dense,*
> *my very life's measure*

Kairos, *notch of arrow in flight,*
degree of my contingency
NOW—which will become never, or ever,
but to say that is to turn away from now,
the real, the only known, the partly known,
unknown in which we wander.

At the distant end of possibility, the other side of time,
redeemer from time,
sharing this prison yet never enclosed,
liberator and inescapable, there is —
YOU.

These two, sometimes, are the range
of all sensing, all experience —
NOW,
the claw that pulls me away from knowing
drags me toward mystery toward death;
YOU,
who sent the arrow flying, are its target.

Yet this now is You. You are this now.

WHAT NOW?

Life will hand us the musical score.
our assignment is to perform it,
quite literally, to play it —
as instrumentalist
or as actor.

But not as game.

It's not that serious.

Nobody is keeping score,
winning is not the purpose.
The playing
is winning.

WHAT WE SAY . . .

We say, "Alas, I cannot do what I once did,"
and keep insisting on doing what we did.

We ask, "Why do I have these limitations?"
forgetting old limits and demands.

We say, "I followed all the directions. Why didn't it work?"
but we knew the answers were never absolute.

We say, "This wasn't where I was heading"
forgetting we chose and we chose and we chose again
and are not at the end of our choosing.

We say, "I carry loss, and loneliness, and sometimes pain"
forgetting lack, and ambiguity, and young hurt.

We say, "I can't go forward; age raises obstacles"
but we went through, over, around young bars.

We say, "This time of life is grievous"
as if we never learned that life is grievous,
full of wonder and risk, of sudden light and sudden darkness,
and they all lead to mystery.

We say, "I feel time slipping by. I don't know how much
is left." We never did.

YAHRTZEIT

Each of us marks a yahrtzeit
as a people marks the anniversary of defeat —
a Pearl Harbor. Although we recovered ground lost
we were never the same after. We never will be.

It led to long conflict. Some of it still goes on.
The ultimate outcome was peace, but after long pain,
struggle, labor. No victory is total.

Always there are buildings missing, stained glass
shattered, neighborhoods vanished, wounds in earth
that nature will heal, but not soon.

Some scars we tend in order to remember
what we lost, and what it was
we had. Death is not retroactive.

Growing years are over but not erased. Death
is either an enemy who must in time prevail, or
an ally whom we cannot recognize.

A *yahrtzeit*, literally "year-time," anniversary of a death, is observed in synagogue services by reciting the mourners' *kaddish*.

CODA

Old age is the time for poetry—not what your teachers used to call poetry and not a printed shape, but poetry defined by what it talks about and how it does it. I think of prose as observation tempered by experience, of poetry as experience tempered by observation.

Now I let myself confront mystery—from mystery I come, through the mystery of the world's grandeur and loveliness, all the way to awe. I let myself touch whatever has set alight in me anything akin to the glory outside me. This is matter of poetry, this is matter of wonder. It doesn't have to be a big wonder. Little ones can make poetry as well as vast ones.

Sometimes this has something to do with religion, often not. Religion can get in the way of wonder. If I'm standing in front of Angel Glacier on Mount Edith Cavell, being told that God made it doesn't increase my wonder any more than being told how water acts at low temperature. God's creating it doesn't explain my response, to the glacier or to the fact that my race produces people like Edith Cavell, and is compelled to remember. When I hear Itzhak Perlman play the Bruch violin concerto, mathematical frequencies of sound are not what I'm responding to. What makes a violin sound like that? How does a composer create what the sounds add up to?

I can easily believe God has a part in this (I assume creating wonders to be his profession) but how—and why—do the fiddler and composer make it happen? Here is a marvel, this ability of human beings to transcend the limits of minds and bodies, using those bodies and minds to do it. My response is kin to their making, and isn't subject to loss in old age.

This awe is not what we usually call religion, though perhaps we should. The perception of the transcendent may have little to do with your asking for your daily needs, but it has much to do with the giving that is beyond all asking. Call Him what name you will; it won't be His name, and it won't matter.

For myself, I am most comfortable calling Him simply: You. When I stand in front of a mountain or an ocean, confront birth or death or a saint, it is not the time for dogma. It is not the time for doubt, either, but don't worry about that. The doubt is seldom empty if you dare it.

In old age, you can re-experience the presences that led to this. Maybe you didn't have time for wonder, for awe, in the busy years. Now you do. Now you will bring all your life into the unexplained and unexplainable light, and see it new, if you are wise. Past days were your gifts to yourself, saved for this time.

When you begin to remember facts, events, names—stop. Let yourself quietly and gently *experience* them. If you weep because a fire has gone out, it may be your tears that have quenched it; if you weep because it is warm and it is beautiful, it is still yours, burning through time.

This may be what old age is made for.

The Author

APPENDIX

Suggested program for formation of a mutual support group:

Several years ago, I went to live in an apartment complex designed for the elderly, a place which was attractive and convenient, offered many services of assistance, and where lived many people undergoing severe, often traumatic, life change. Even by middle-age (however you define it) people make many changes, and live with changes that were made for them, but in old age, changes come faster and thicker, and seem to be more severe. In the place where I lived, there were some exceedingly depressed people. The managership of the complex was concerned about these tenants and I shared their concern.

It had seemed to me that, speaking very generally, "ethnic" populations in this country tend to have inherent support systems, a particular kind of belonging their members can find wherever they go. There is undoubtedly good reason for this, since they have long shared a "non-belonging." I know of nothing like this in the general population, in which transfer to a new location can leave one totally alien.

The only exception seems to be the close fellowship known as Alcoholics Anonymous, those who have suffered the experiences, social, emotional, and spiritual, of alcoholism, and embraced a shared program of recovery and of personal growth.

Possibly to a lesser degree, this is true of other fellowships made up of people dealing with specific life-stresses. I wondered if something similar, a shared program of structured emotional and spiritual way of life, might be helpful for the depressed, the sick, the bewildered, the anxious, in the place where I lived, and possibly elsewhere. Certainly that housing complex was not

215

unique in its tenancy.

The situations are not totally analogous, for old age is not an illness to recover from, and while depression is, like alcoholism, an illness, it is different in kind. Still, the sharing of a common disability (if I can call either one that) might offer what nothing else could. Advice from a fellow-senior would, I knew, come much more welcome than the same advice from the young, who wouldn't "know what it is like." This would be true even of skilled professionals who were young and energetic.

AA has not chalked up its record of successful recoveries just because its members have the same problems (they don't have *exactly* the same ones), or because "misery loves company." At the heart of its life is "The Program," a remarkably effective (some say "inspired") philosophy of life based on a series of steps which are mentally and emotionally, but primarily spiritually, therapeutic. It is the program which is so life-changing when put into practice.

This program is the basis for most of the countless other fellowships that have arisen to address the personality problems and needs prevalent in our culture.

My question was whether a similar philosophy and program of mutual support might be useful in the milieu of old age.

To make the story short, that idea has been put into practice and continued for some time in that setting, and I'm told is in practice in a similar place on the east coast.

It suffered through trials and errors, it evidenced differences in how it ought to be conducted. But I saw, in a couple of years, some remarkable life-enhancements brought about, some bonding done in its context that would not otherwise have come about. I saw some healthy changes in lives.

It started with the idea of help for dealing with problems of old age, then that turned into dealing with depression. That was too narrow; it eventuated into calling itself a way of dealing with disruptive change, of any kind. That isn't a matter of age.

It seems to me it is still worth trying, worth improving, worth the trials and errors it will undoubtedly engender.

POSSIBILITY OF THE FORMATION
OF SUPPORT GROUPS, to provide:

- sharing of a regular time and place to talk, and listen to one another, where one's hearers relate by experience, to what is said.

- a carefully-thought-out program for growth and self-knowledge. This might be similar to existing 12-step programs, with models for traditions, aims, etc drawn from these, but adapted. A possible program, not necessarily in this order:

1. I will learn to separate ideas and opinions, remembering that not all values are of equal importance, and that nothing is bad or good *because* it is new; nothing is good or bad *because* it is old.

2. I will regularly take a moral inventory of myself. [See below—there should be guidelines for this.]

3. I am responsible for the health of my own body, mind, and spirit. I will be honest with my physician, my counselors, and myself.

4. I will be willing to ask for help; I am willing to accept and use help offered.

5. I will remember that life has always expected me to change. I have changed in the past, so I know I can change now.

6. I will try to understand my own needs and wants, and the difference between them.

7. I will be aware of my resources. [There might be a guide for inventory of these.]

8. I will remember that God works through people, events, and opportunities. He expects me to make use of them.

I reviewed the steps used by Alcoholics Anonymous and other 12-step mutual support groups and movements. I think it is important to use whatever steps we find needed, without requiring that they number 12. For this situation, some traditional ones may be inapplicable, even as adapted, but I think they all work.

There is good reason for the AA steps to be put in the past tense. For this purpose, however, it seemed to me the present tense or past imperfect, dealing with continuing action, worked better.

A rough draft of such adaptation of the traditional might be:

1. We admit we are powerless over the changes time brings about, and are willing to accept this new stage of life.

2. We have come to believe that a power greater than ourselves can restore us to dignity, humility, and the knowledge of our own worth as unique human beings.

3. We make a decision to turn our will and our lives over to the care of God as we understand him.

4. We make a searching and fearless moral inventory of ourselves, recognizing our part in producing our loneliness and in any strained relationships.

5. We admit to God, to ourselves, and to another human being the exact nature of our contributions to our own unhappiness.

6. We are entirely ready to have God remove our defects of character.

7. We humbly ask him to remove our shortcomings.

8. We have made a list of all persons we had harmed, and become willing to make amends to them all.

9. We make direct amends to such people whenever possible, except when to do so would injure them or others.

10. We continue to take personal inventory and when we are wrong promptly admit it.

11. We seek through prayer and meditation to improve our conscious contact with God as we understand him, praying only for knowledge of his will for us and the power to carry that out.

12. Having had a spiritual awakening as the result of these steps, we try to carry this message to others, and to practice these principles in all our affairs.